Shaken
FOUNDATIONS

Shaken FOUNDATIONS

Sermons from America's Pulpits after the Terrorist Attacks

David P. Polk, Editor

CHALICE
PRESS

ST. LOUIS, MISSOURI

© Copyright 2001 by Chalice Press

Biblical quotations, unless otherwise noted, are from the *New Revised Standard Version Bible*, copyright 1989, Division of Christian Education of the National Council of the Churches of Christ in the United States of America. Used by permission. All rights reserved.

Scripture quotations marked (NIV) are taken from the HOLY BIBLE, NEW INTERNATIONAL VERSION®. NIV®. Copyright © 1973, 1978, 1984 by International Bible Society. Used by permission of Zondervan Publishing House. All rights resrved.

> All royalties derived from the sale of *Shaken Foundations* will go to the Domestic Terrorism Appeal of Church World Service.

Cover photos: Steve Skjold. Lower left photo detail from vigil at St. Paul Unity Church, St. Paul, Minn., on Sept. 11, 2001. Other cover photos from a memorial service at the state capitol in St. Paul, Minn., on Sept. 16, 2001.
Cover design: Michael A. Domínguez
Interior design: Elizabeth Wright
Art direction: Michael A. Domínguez

This book is printed on acid-free, recycled paper.

Visit Chalice Press on the World Wide Web at
www.chalicepress.com

10 9 8 7 6 5 4 3 2 1   01 02 03 04 05 06

Library of Congress Cataloging–in–Publication Data

Shaken foundations : sermons from America's pulpits after the terrorist attacks / David P. Polk, ed.
    p.   cm.
    ISBN 0-8272-3453-8
    1. September 11 Terrorist Attacks, 2001—Sermons.   2. Sermons, American—21st century.   I. Polk, David Patrick.
BT736.15 .S43 2001
252—dc21   2001007041

Printed in the United States of America

Contents

Foreword

It happened before our very eyes—that moment that shattered the illusion of our inviolability and altered the landscape of our social wellbeing from this time forward. One plane crashing into the north tower of New York's World Trade Center—that could be an accident...couldn't it? Then, with television cameras riveted on the smoking skyscraper amid mounting concern for unknown numbers trapped inside...the gut-wrenching sight of another jet coming in from the right, followed by an explosion of fire shooting out from the other side of the south tower.

No, this was no unfortunate accident that we were watching. In that chilling moment, we knew: Nothing would ever be quite the same again. In a demonic twist on those ancient initials designating a Christian "hinge of history," B.C. and A.D. had a perverse new reference in our present lives: Before Crash. After Disaster.

Millions of us saw the scene played out over and again, from various angles. Real time. Slow motion. Freeze frame. As if the ending could be altered. As if the outcome, this time—surely this time; please, God this time!—would be different. But no. This was no simulation game with multiple possibilities. One very destructive, very deadly set of possibilities had already been made real. The jet slashing into solid steel and concrete like a knife into warm butter slashed through our fragile barriers against the terror of the unimaginable as well. It is not only the horizon of lower Manhattan that now has a gaping hole. So do our hearts.

It is safe to say that on the following Sunday, every sermon from every pulpit all across America, from every spectrum of

Christian belief, tried to help the bewildered faithful—preachers included—begin to gain some sense of perspective on the events of September 11.

This volume presents a diverse sampling of those efforts. Beginning in New York and Washington but reaching well out into the heartland of America, and continuing into the following weeks, voices of healing and hope and compassion and, yes, confrontation—with evil and its perpetrators—pierced the veil of darkness. To collect all those words deserving of our attention would require a resource of unfathomable enormity. These are but a representation.

There was one word. One Word. The prologue of the good news according to John tells of that Word becoming flesh and dwelling among us, in Jesus of Nazareth. The narrative goes on to talk of that incarnate Word as "light." "And the light shines in the darkness," we are told—"and the darkness has not overcome it."

A sobering, but at the same time reassuring, claim on John's part. We want, we expect, we *ache* for the line to read: "The light shines in the darkness, and overwhelms it. Overpowers it. *Obliterates* it!" No more darkness of sin and evil. Only the triumphant light of goodness and love.

But that is not what we are promised. What we are promised is that no matter how devastating the darkness that seems at times to envelop us, no matter how cruel the inhumanity, that darkness *cannot blot out the light!* We saw it, time and again. The selfless acts of compassion. Those firefighters. The caregivers. Blood donors. Strangers carrying the immobilized down dozens of flights of stairs to safety. Where, indeed, was God on September 11? Need you ask? Not in the calamity, but in the zillion little (and not so little) acts of resurrection that came during and after.

Yes, the foundations have been shaken, and they are shaking still. But they endure. Praise be to God, they do endure.

David P. Polk

Acknowledgments

Appreciation is expressed to each of the contributors to this volume, who have waived any share of royalties so that all such proceeds may be designated for disaster relief.

The collection came together quickly with the considerable assistance of my colleague at Chalice Press, Jon Berquist, who surfaced a number of candidates for inclusion while hard at work editing a companion volume of essays, *Strike Terror No More: Theological and Ethical Responses to America's New War*; and equally of J. Richard Butler, assistant to the president of Union Theological Seminary in New York, who reached out successfully to various of Union's distinguished alums in securing sermon texts from throughout the greater New York area. I also wish to thank Barbara Lundblad, A. M. Pennybacker, and my editorial assistant, Laura Christian, for their help on this project, as well as all the staff at Christian Board of Publication who ensured that this made it into print on a very accelerated schedule.

What Do We Need to Dust Off?

Daniel Paul Matthews

The Rev. Dr. Daniel Paul Matthews is rector of the parish of Trinity Church, Wall Street, a historic Episcopal congregation so close to the World Trade Center that its building is still closed due to damage from the devastation. This sermon was delivered during a parish eucharist held in the Trinity parish's temporary place of worship at the Shrine of St. Elizabeth Seton, State Street, Manhattan, on September 23, 2001. Trinity's church building was inaccessible, in the "red zone" controlled by emergency management authorities.

Dust. Dust. Everywhere. Everywhere, everywhere, everywhere, dust, dust. Everything covered in dust. Unbelievable. We couldn't imagine how the whole of south Manhattan Island could become covered in dust.

What do we need to dust off?

It wasn't long before we began saying, "What should we dust off first? What should be the priority in getting rid of some of the dust?" And we decided the first thing was the pews. So people could come in and sit down and rest and pray and reflect and receive some counseling.

1

What next?

Well, what about the prayer books? People need to pick up the prayer books and look at them and find the prayer that speaks to them at this moment. Dust! Dust the prayer books.

What next?

The votive candles. Of course. There will be people coming in who will want to light a candle for someone who has died or someone who is missing. Dust, dust the votive candles.

And we're still dusting.

But the dust did not just fall in the southern tip of Manhattan. The dust fell all over the whole world on September 11. Not one inch of this Earth is without dust. Little villages all over the world, people, religious groups, faiths of all traditions, nations—everybody is covered with the dust of the World Trade Center. None is without dust.

Of course, they're saying the same thing we said: What do we dust off first? What do we need right now? What's most important to us? What do we need to use immediately?

And what's secondary? And what's not very important?

Not only are we saying that in this city; it is being said around the world. Because the world has changed. Values are beginning to be different. People are saying, "What do we need to dust off, and what do we need to keep?" You and I are saying the same thing. What about your life? What about my life? What about our lives? What is important to dust off, right now, to preserve and keep and use? And what seems superficial and empty?

Oh yes. We're all asking these questions.

Have you ever been in an antique store? They're fun places to visit. You walk in and see all this stuff from bygone times, things that are old fashioned. And then maybe if you're interested enough, the owner says, "If you'd really like to see a lot of things, out in the back is a big barn. Would you like to go in?" And you say, "Sure, I'd like to see your barn of antiques."

So he wanders out behind the shop, unlocks the big padlock, and opens the doors. He begins turning on all the lights, and the place is full of things from bygone eras, all covered with dust.

You say to yourself, *I wonder if anybody's been in here in years? Look at everything, so covered in dust that you can hardly tell what it is.* You can't tell one thing from another. You begin to wander through and try to discern what you are seeing.

You come across a table that has something on it and you say, "That looks like what my grandfather used to use. I haven't seen one since he died." You pick it up, reach in your pocket, pull out your handkerchief, and begin to dust it off. As you dust, you realize that it is exactly what your grandfather had in his house. You smile and say, "No matter what it costs, I'm going to buy it, because it reminds me of him, and it bespeaks my traditions and who I really am and who my grandfather was." As you leave the barn, you look around and say, "Such a treasure among so much junk."

That's what some of us feel like, isn't it? What are our treasures? What are those things that really matter? Some of them are covered with dust, and we're trying to dust and polish them because they are valuable treasures. These treasures are not things, some of them are people, some of them are ideas, and some of them are beliefs.

We are a people eager to find out what matters and what doesn't, what's true and what's false. The value systems we hold are being adjusted.

In the midst of this crisis, the president called for prayers and ringing of bells at noon on Friday, September 14. I got hold of Jim Doran and Mike Borrero, the two engineers who maintain Trinity and St. Paul's, and asked if they could ring the bells. Mike said, "Dr. Matthews, I'm sorry, we can't possibly do that. You can't imagine what it's like down here."

About an hour later, Mike was on the phone and said, "Guess what? We got in the church, I crawled up the bell tower, I picked up an iron bar and beat the hell out of the bell. And when I got back down, they told me that all the police officers, the firemen, and the volunteers heard that bell, took their hats off in silence, and stood, as if to say, "The Lord God reigns even in this hell."

The Lord God does reign. God willing, we'll ring the bell at St. Paul's at 12 o'clock every day as long as we exist, remembering to announce that to the world.

At times like this, a bell becomes more than just a bell; it becomes a sacrament. In a moment we'll have bread and a little wine. Simple. It's not just bread and wine, it's a sacrament saying, God loves me and God loves you, and God gave Himself to you and to me.

We'll never forget the voice of the man speaking to his wife from that doomed plane over Pennsylvania, words that you and I need to dust off and say more often: I love you, I love you, I love you. We know that nothing's more profound for that widow, and nothing is more profound for you and me, than to know that God loves us, and that we love each other.

I have my own symbol, my sacrament.

When that smoke was so thick and we thought we were going to die—we all admit it now—someone handed me a mask. I can't tell you what a treasure it was. I've worn it every day when I've been near Ground Zero. I'm going to save it because it means life to me. A little, inexpensive mask. Lots of simple things are meaning a lot more to you and to me than they ever have before. Maybe someday my grandchild will find it and say, "My grandfather wore this and it saved his life, back in 2001."

Providence has a way with us at a time like this. I want to read the Collect for today. It's such a powerful Collect for this particular moment. I hope you'll make a copy of it and put it on your refrigerator and say it every time you grab that refrigerator door. Listen to how profoundly prophetic and appropriate these words are for you and for me:

Grant us, Lord, not to be anxious about earthly things, but to love things heavenly; and even now, while we are placed among things that are passing away, to hold fast to that which shall endure; through Jesus Christ Our Lord, let us say together: Amen.

On This Day of Prayer and Remembrance

President George W. Bush

George W. Bush is President of the United States of America. These remarks were delivered at the prayer service at Washington National Cathedral on Friday, September 14, 2001, designated a National Day of Prayer and Remembrance.

We are here in the middle hour of our grief. So many have suffered so great a loss, and today we express our nation's sorrow. We come before God to pray for the missing and the dead, and for those who loved them.

On Tuesday, our country was attacked with deliberate and massive cruelty. We have seen the images of fire and ashes and bent steel.

Now come the names, the list of casualties we are only beginning. They are the names of men and women who began their day at a desk or in an airport, busy with life. They are the names of people who faced death and in their last moments called home to say, "Be brave, and I love you."

They are the names of passengers who defied their murderers and prevented the murder of others on the ground. They are the names of men and women who wore the uniform of the United States and died at their posts.

They are the names of rescuers—the ones whom death found running up the stairs and into the fires to help others. We will read all these names. We will linger over them and learn their stories, and many Americans will weep.

To the children and parents and spouses and families and friends of the lost, we offer the deepest sympathy of the nation. And I assure you, you are not alone.

Just three days removed from these events, Americans do not yet have the distance of history, but our responsibility to history is already clear: to answer these attacks and rid the world of evil.

War has been waged against us by stealth and deceit and murder.

This nation is peaceful, but fierce when stirred to anger. This conflict was begun on the timing and terms of others; it will end in a way and at an hour of our choosing.

Our purpose as a nation is firm, yet our wounds as a people are recent and unhealed and lead us to pray. In many of our prayers this week, there's a searching and an honesty. At St. Patrick's Cathedral in New York, on Tuesday, a woman said, "I pray to God to give us a sign that he's still here."

Others have prayed for the same, searching hospital to hospital, carrying pictures of those still missing.

God's signs are not always the ones we look for. We learn in tragedy that his purposes are not always our own, yet the prayers of private suffering, whether in our homes or in this great cathedral, are known and heard and understood.

There are prayers that help us last through the day or endure the night. There are prayers of friends and strangers that give us strength for the journey, and there are prayers that yield our will to a will greater than our own.

This world He created is of moral design. Grief and tragedy and hatred are only for a time. Goodness, remembrance, and love have no end, and the Lord of life holds all who die and all who mourn.

It is said that adversity introduces us to ourselves. This is true of a nation as well. In this trial, we have been reminded and the world has seen that our fellow Americans are generous and kind, resourceful and brave.

We see our national character in rescuers working past exhaustion, in long lines of blood donors, in thousands of citizens who have asked to work and serve in any way possible. And we have seen our national character in eloquent acts of sacrifice. Inside the World Trade Center, one man who could have saved himself stayed until the end and at the side of his quadriplegic friend. A beloved priest died giving the last rites to a firefighter. Two office workers, finding a disabled stranger, carried her down sixty-eight floors to safety.

A group of men drove through the night from Dallas to Washington to bring skin grafts for burned victims. In these acts and many others, Americans showed a deep commitment to one another and an abiding love for our country.

Today, we feel what Franklin Roosevelt called "the warm courage of national unity." This is a unity of every faith and every background. This has joined together political parties and both houses of Congress. It is evident in services of prayer and candlelight vigils and American flags, which are displayed in pride and waved in defiance. Our unity is a kinship of grief and a steadfast resolve to prevail against our enemies. And this unity against terror is now extending across the world.

America is a nation full of good fortune, with so much to be grateful for, but we are not spared from suffering. In every generation, the world has produced enemies of human freedom. They have attacked America because we are freedom's home and defender, and the commitment of our fathers is now the calling of our time.

On this national day of prayer and remembrance, we ask almighty God to watch over our nation and grant us patience and resolve in all that is to come. We pray that He will comfort and console those who now walk in sorrow. We thank Him for each life we now must mourn and the promise of a life to come.

As we've been assured, neither death, nor life, nor angels, nor principalities, nor powers, nor things present, nor things to come, nor height, nor depth can separate us from God's love.

May He bless the souls of the departed. May He comfort our own. And may He always guide our country.

God bless America.

How Firm a Foundation!

Billy Graham

Billy Graham is undoubtedly the most widely renowned Christian evangelist of our time. This message was delivered at the prayer service at Washington National Cathedral on Friday, September 14, 2001, designated a National Day of Prayer and Remembrance.

President and Mrs. Bush, I want to say a personal word on behalf of many people. Thank you, Mr. President, for calling this Day of Prayer and Remembrance. We needed it at this time.

We come together today to affirm our conviction that God cares for us, whatever our ethnic, religious, or political backgrounds may be.

The Bible says that God is "the God of all comfort, who comforts us in all our troubles."

No matter how hard we try, words simply cannot express the horror, the shock, and the revulsion we all feel over what took place in this nation on Tuesday morning. September 11 will go down in our history as a day to remember.

Today we say to those who masterminded this cruel plot, and to those who carried it out, that the spirit of this nation will not be defeated by their twisted and diabolical schemes. Some day those responsible will be brought to justice, as President Bush and our Congress have so forcefully stated.

But today, we especially come together in this service to confess our need of God. We've always needed God from the very beginning of this nation, but today we need Him especially. We're facing a new kind of enemy. We're involved in a new kind of warfare, and we need the help of the Spirit of God. The Bible's words are our hope: "God is our refuge and strength, an ever-present help in trouble. Therefore we will not fear, though the earth give way and the mountains fall into the heart of the sea" (Psalm 46:1–2, NIV).

But how do we understand something like this? Why does God allow evil like this to take place? Perhaps that is what you are asking now. You may even be angry at God. I want to assure you that God understands these feelings that you may have.

We've seen so much on our televisions, heard on our radios, stories that bring tears to our eyes and make us all feel a sense of anger. But God can be trusted, even when life seems at its darkest.

But what are some of the lessons we can learn?

First, we are reminded of the mystery and reality of evil.

I have been asked hundreds of times in my life why God allows tragedy and suffering. I have to confess that I really do not know the answer totally, even to my own satisfaction. I have to accept, by faith, that God is sovereign, and He's a God of love and mercy and compassion in the midst of suffering. The Bible says that God is not the author of evil. It speaks of evil as a "mystery." In 2 Thessalonians 2:7 it talks about the mystery of iniquity. The Old Testament prophet Jeremiah said, "The heart is deceitful above all things and beyond cure. Who can understand it?" He asked that question, "Who can understand it?" And that's one reason we each need God in our lives.

The lesson of this event is not only about the mystery of iniquity and evil, but secondly, it's a lesson about our need for each other.

What an example New York and Washington have been to the world these past few days! None of us will ever forget the pictures of our courageous firefighters and police, many of whom have lost friends and colleagues, or the hundreds of people attending or standing patiently in line to donate blood. A tragedy like this could have torn our country apart, but instead it has united us, and we've become a family. So those perpetrators who took this on to tear us apart, it has worked the other way. It's backlashed, it's backfired. We are more united than ever before. I think this was exemplified in a very moving way when the members of our congress stood shoulder to shoulder the other day and sang "God Bless America."

Finally, difficult as it may be for us to see right now, this event can give a message of hope—hope for the present and hope for the future.

Yes, there is hope. There's hope for the present, because I believe the stage has already been set for a new spirit in our nation.

One of the things we desperately need is a spiritual renewal in this country. We need a spiritual revival in America. And God has told us in His Word, time after time, that we are to repent of our sins and we're to turn to Him and He will bless us in a new way.

But there is also hope for the future because of God's promises. As a Christian, I have hope, not just for this life, but for heaven and the life to come. And many of those people who died this past week are in heaven right now, and they wouldn't want to come back. It's so glorious and so wonderful. And that's the hope for all of us who put our faith in God. I pray that you will have this hope in your heart.

This event reminds us of the brevity and the uncertainty of life. We never know when we too will be called into eternity. I doubt if even one of those people who got on those planes or walked into the World Trade Center or the Pentagon last Tuesday morning thought it would be the last day of their lives. It didn't occur to them. And that's why each of us needs to face our own spiritual needs and commit ourselves to God and His will now.

Here in this majestic National Cathedral we see all around us symbols of the cross. For the Christian—I'm speaking for the Christian now—the cross tells us that God understands our sin and our suffering, for He took upon Himself in the person of Jesus Christ our sins and our suffering. And from the cross God declares, "I love you. I know the heartaches and the sorrows and the pains that you feel. But I love you."

The story does not end with the cross, for Easter points us beyond the tragedy of the cross to the empty tomb. It tells us that there is hope for eternal life, for Christ has conquered evil and death and hell. Yes, there is hope.

I've become an old man now, and I've preached all over the world, and the older I get the more I cling to that hope that I started with many years ago and proclaimed in many languages to many parts of the world.

Several years ago at the National Prayer Breakfast here in Washington, Ambassador Andrew Young (who had just gone through the tragic death of his wife) closed his talk with a quote from the old hymn "How Firm a Foundation."

We all watched in horror as planes crashed into the steel and glass of the World Trade Center. Those majestic towers, built on solid foundations, were examples of the prosperity and creativity of America. When damaged, those buildings eventually plummeted to the ground, imploding in upon themselves. Yet underneath the debris is a foundation that was not destroyed. Therein lies the truth of that old hymn that Andrew Young quoted, "How Firm a Foundation."

Yes, our nation has been attacked, buildings destroyed, lives lost. But now we have a choice: whether to implode and disintegrate emotionally and spiritually as a people and a nation, or whether we choose to become stronger through all of this struggle, to rebuild on a solid foundation. And I believe that we are in the process of starting to rebuild on that foundation. That foundation is our trust in God. That's what this service is all about, and in that faith we have the strength to endure something as difficult and horrendous as what we have experienced this week.

This has been a terrible week with many tears, but it also has been a week of great faith. Churches all across the country have called prayer meetings, and today is a day that they are celebrating not only in this country but in many parts of the world.

And in the words of that familiar hymn that Andrew Young quoted—it says:

Fear not, I am with thee; O be not dismayed,
For I am thy God, and will still give thee aid;
I'll strengthen thee, help thee, and cause thee to stand,
Upheld by my righteous, omnipotent hand.

My prayer today is that we will feel the loving arms of God wrapped around us and will know in our hearts that God will never forsake us as we trust in Him.

We also know that God is going to give wisdom and courage and strength to the President and those around him. And this is going to be a day that we will remember as a day of victory.

May God bless you all.

Finding What Is Lost

Nathan D. Baxter

The Very Reverend Nathan D. Baxter is Dean of the Washington National Cathedral. This sermon was preached there on Sunday, September 16, 2001.

A lost sheep. A lost coin. The gospel reading today is about possessions lost. Precious, valuable, essential possessions lost in the mundane routines of daily work and living. A shepherd with a small flock of one hundred sheep, whose livelihood depends upon the survival of each one of his sheep. And a homeowner who loses a very valuable piece of currency. She knows well her domestic economics and that she cannot survive without that very valuable coin.

In these parables Jesus teaches us how to respond to the emotional and spiritual crises such essential losses can present in human lives. What are the lessons? First, the shepherd leaves the ninety-nine and searches for the one. When the essential things of life are lost, it requires our full attention and commitment—a willingness to lay aside other priorities to focus on the most essential qualities that are lost.

Secondly, the parable of the lost coin teaches that spiritual light is required to find what is lost. We need illumined those nooks and crannies of life that our normal patterns of daily observation would miss—the blind spots too dark for our natural power of sight.

Yes, like the shepherd and the householder, the American soul has lost precious and essential possessions in the attacks upon our symbols of economic vitality and military power—the Trade Towers and the Pentagon. Amid the rubble of steel, glass, and human bodies there is something of our soul that is lost for the living: a sense of security and a sense of justice. There is now a vulnerability that we feel as everyday Americans; a sense that we and those we love cannot be protected from foreign aggression. A fear that we and those we love are now forever vulnerable to the evil of terror, destruction, and mass violence at work and home.

Last week I had the opportunity to make a pastoral visit regarding this tragedy with the children in our cathedral elementary school, Beauvoir. I tried to allow them to talk about what was on their hearts: what they had seen and heard; what they were thinking and feeling. They talked about the terrible loss of life—which included mommies and daddies and little children. They talked about the bad people making bad things happen.

Finally, I asked them: "What did the 'bad people' want to make happen by these attacks?" From everywhere in that assembly came the statement, "They want us to be afraid!" There was no hesitation. They knew instantly the intent, for they felt it, as do we: the vulnerability, uncertainty, anxiety, apprehensiveness. But they also spoke about the good people who were risking their lives to help others, especially firemen and police and medical personnel. They were beginning to see what St. Paul taught, that "Where evil is present, goodness is even more greatly present" (Romans 5:20, author trans.). And what St. John taught, "The light shines in the darkness, and the darkness did not overcome it" (John 1:5).

The purpose in dastardly, evil acts, such as war against innocent civilians, is to impose fear—fear that blinds us to everything but the evil and darkness, fear that disrupts our spiritual capacity to go on with life as an open democracy, as a generous people, as a free, confident, and progressive productive society in everyday living.

But even as we see glimpses of goodness, we still have lost our sense of impregnability. If we are to reclaim it, we must now lay aside such things as our assumed privileges of so many public conveniences and free access (I will never again complain about the inconvenience of security in airports—please search me and the guy behind me).

But also, we must lay aside the quick, potent energy of blind rage and revenge that can only power us to make hasty judgments. If in the weeks and months ahead we do not find the strength to lay aside such negative energy, we will become a society of emotional and spiritual cripples.

On the day of the attack, an Israeli teacher said to a *Washington Post* reporter: "I feel sad because now the Americans will be like us—scared, angry, not safe. I always thought of America as some sort of a Disneyland, innocent, naive, and childlike, a place that didn't have all the scars that we have. Now [I'm afraid] they'll be cynical like us and they'll start looking for revenge, like we do."

On the one hand, we have never been a people to live long with cynicism and vengeance. Somehow in our history we have found our way through such mire. Yet we have never in our history had to live with the insecurity of terrorism. But people of faith who have lived in cultures of terror with whom I have talked—Israelis, Palestinians, South Africans, Liberians, Irish—all say it is their faith, above all else, that keeps them focused, secure in spirit, and hopeful for justice rather than revenge.

I am impressed that, though our President is clearly angry, he is consistent in saying he seeks justice and not revenge. He has resisted ill-informed and hasty action for retribution and is consulting in accountable ways with other nations—building accountable partnerships to destroy this evil. I pray that we continue to seek divine wisdom and courage to keep to this course.

I think he and his advisers understand—and we must understand—that justice is never "just about us," no matter what the tragedy of our experience. When it is just about us it becomes vengeance and blind retribution, and more innocents suffer. The human aspect of this work is not necessarily always passive or nonviolent. But true justice is never about revenge, never about pure retribution or acting without the light of our spiritual values and accountability to the larger community. We must not become the evil we deplore in the search for justice.

Justice is used in our everyday secular language in courts, police work, and civil rights pursuits. But justice is a biblical word, a word of religious faith sometimes translated "righteousness." It means the work of repairing God's vision for a broken world. It is about making decisions and taking actions that are intended for healing, restoration, wholeness, and peace for human community.

I believe that the search for justice, in the light of the gospel, means more than destroying the cells of assassins and terrorists. In the long view, I believe it means that we must ask why we are hated in some countries, some of whom we will need as partners to confront this enemy. Perhaps the light of truth will help us reexamine some of our policies and attitudes over the years that have appeared arrogant and insensitive to less powerful countries and even some allies. I have no question but that many decisions were seen as in the best strategic interests of America. But power and invincibility have a way of making us blind to the interest and dignity of others. It can give us the privilege of being insensitive to the realities of their daily lives.

An Arab student in Jerusalem said, "Now the Americans won't judge us. Now they'll get it—that these terrorists, all of them, aren't human beings. They'll do anything. Maybe [the U.S.] won't be so quick to condemn [all of] us. It is easy for them to be self-righteous when [terror] didn't affect them."

This is why at a time like this we turn to religious faith, because our spirituality helps us to be in touch with our deeper beliefs, our deeper values. This does not mean that our feelings of anger, rage, and suspicion will easily go away. These are very natural and human responses to tragedy. But true faith is the discipline that helps us to say, "Evil has caused this unconscionable tragedy, and I do not want my pain to make me another tool of that evil."

A local Muslim Imam told me last week that a Sikh man was attacked on the street. As they attacked, the assailants were calling their victim a "murderous Muslim." The attackers saw a turban and assumed that any Eastern Asian must be a Muslim. American democracy is a beautiful, complex mosaic of colors, cultures, religions, and races. My brothers and sisters, in the weeks and months to come, the gravity of this tragedy will continue to unfold and the pain will increase. We must resist turning on one another.

We must remember that evil does not wear a turban, a tunic, a yarmulke, or a cross. Evil wears the garment of a human heart, a garment woven from the threads of hate and fear. I fear those Christian leaders who accuse other Americans who do not share their political and moral views as culprits for this tragedy; or who say that America is so wicked that God has allowed this to happen. Yes, we have our sins and failings, but this is a good nation of good people of good heart. That goodness comes from our deep faith in God and democracy. It is this light, this faith that will give us the strength to find justice with integrity.

Speaking of faith in God, I am also aware that many feel they are losing their faith because they are so angry with God. True spirituality helps us not only to mourn but gives a healing voice to our rage and pain. Anger with God is an act of faith. We do not rail against that which we do not believe exists. We do not rail if we do not think that there is the potential for God to be affected by our passion, our grief, our pain. We rail against God because we believe that God is just by nature and has sinned by not eliminating the potential evil of free will. Anger, hatred toward God, is an act of intimate faith. A marriage counselor once said, "Healthy anger is love frustrated." It is a way for lovers to stay engaged in the midst of grave disappointment.

As a people of faith, what we find in prayer is that, as we beat upon the breast of our seemingly silent, enigmatic God, we are being gently enfolded into the arms of that love which has been frustrated, and our souls begin to heal. And in God's arms the light becomes brighter, enabling us to see the goodness of God in the spirit of good people, risking their very lives for others—people reaching out beyond race, culture and class, religion, and personal safety to confront the tragic effects of evil.

Finally, no matter where you are in your grief and fear, remember that God is the true Shepherd and Householder. God knows that in great tragedy God's children can feel lost, separated from God. But if we will, we can feel God seeking us, reaching out to us, pulling at the strings of our heart. Drawing us even to this cathedral this morning. Drawing us through the fear, anger, grief, and anguish—even our sense of justice lost. Drawing us like a mother to that place in her bosom where there is comfort, goodness, healing, and peace. For our Christian faith assures us that we and those who have died are never lost to God.

St. Paul wrote to the persecuted Christians at Rome: "Who will separate us from the love of Christ? Will hardship, or distress, or persecution, or famine, or nakedness, or peril, or [violent weapons]?…No, in all these things we are more than conquerors through him who loved us. For I am convinced that neither death, nor life, nor angels, nor rulers, nor [fear of] things present, nor things to come, nor [evil] powers, nor height, nor depth [of life], nor anything else in all creation, will be able to separate us from the love of God in Christ Jesus our Lord" (Romans 8:35–39).

Yes, God is the Good Shepherd who will seek us in our tragedy, in our despair, even in our death. The Shepherd finds us, and brings us home to peace. Amen.

Fragments

Barbara K. Lundblad

Barbara Lundblad is the Joe Engle Associate Professor of Preaching at Union Theological Seminary in New York City and a minister in the Evangelical Lutheran Church of America. She delivered this message during a service of holy communion at Union Seminary on Thursday, September 13, two days after the tragedy.

John 6:3, 5–13

"Gather up the fragments left over," said Jesus, "so that nothing may be lost."

We have been trying to do that since Tuesday. Trying to find meaning where there is none. Trying to make pieces fit together that are forever broken. Trying to see the skyline as we remembered it. Trying to gather up the fragments. Some of you hadn't even attended your first class at Union before it was cancelled on Tuesday.

I have not been able to gather the fragments into any meaningful whole. I've turned to the Psalms to cry and rage, and I've stood with Jesus weeping as he looks out over the city. But it was the fragments that led me to John's gospel, to the story of broken bread and fish. "And from the fragments of the gather up the fragments

Prison, ed. Eberhard Bethge,

five barley loaves, left by those who had eaten, they filled twelve baskets." (Evidently, they had eaten all the fish!) John doesn't tell us what the disciples did with all those pieces of bread. Perhaps, after all these centuries, they're still being passed out, even today.

Fragments—that's all I have today, but I have been assured that fragments are something rather than nothing.

Fragment: On Tuesday someone set up a TV in "The Pit," Union's town square and meeting place. That afternoon, Jill Lum brought her daughter to school for the first time. Only four days old, the tiny girl slept soundly, completely unaware of our need to see her and touch her. Jill set the baby carrier on the table so we could gather 'round—amazed at fingernails so perfectly formed at such a young age. A wondrous miracle of life while images of death came at us from the television a few feet away. A double-exposed photograph. How can we gather up the fragments that tell us life goes on even when we fear it will not?

Fragment: Yesterday, an e-mail from my friend Viola Raheb in Bethlehem, passing on a letter from her brother Mitri. She's director of Lutheran schools on the West Bank and he's pastor of the Evangelical Christmas Lutheran Church in Bethlehem. Imagine—Palestinian Lutherans! They shared their deep sorrow and profound grief for the victims of this tragic attack. They also shared their fear and dismay: "Unfortunately, the media has shown scenes of a few Palestinians celebrating this tragedy. We want you to know that these few do not speak for or represent the entire Palestinian people." I give thanks to God that Farid Esack has come from South Africa to be with us this semester to teach "The World of Islams," to talk with us in the hallways, to read from the Koran two days ago when we gathered here raw with fear and grief. Already we have heard the news of Muslim people being attacked, of mosques and schools marred with hateful threats. What can we do as people of faith, primarily Christian, across the street from Jewish Theological Seminary, in a city increasingly Muslim? How can we gather up the

fragments of understanding and hope acros
religious traditions?

Fragment: We have seen the human spirit
ashes, the unfathomable courage of ordinary
carrying a woman who couldn't walk, down fift
safety. "I only knew his name was Louie," she sa
police, and EMTs risking their lives to save oth
give up hope, searching and digging now whi
Long lines around the block at St. Luke's hos
Street—too many people eager to give blood. M
than there are jobs. "Come back tomorrow." Hov
up fragments of determination and courage to f
that must be done to mend our city?

Fragment: Waking or sleeping, we cannot
out of our minds—the towers that shaped the sky
us find our bearings. The towers where I stood
and dad from an Iowa farm, looking down in wo
buses far below, at the city spread out to the no
with the lamp in the harbor. The solid, shining to
into dust. But we knew without speaking that tl
not empty: They were filled with people. From nov
speak as we have spoken before. Never again c
language of "surgical strikes" or "collateral damag
on, we must speak of people. How can we g
fragments—the photos of the missing—an
compassion to those beyond our shores whose f
be posted on the walls and lampposts of our city

Fragment: Yesterday some of you headed d
knowing what to do. The blood banks were fille
Cross didn't know what to do with you. So yo
people were gathering—Union Square Park. The
and sang and talked with those who were searcl
ones. Soon forty others joined you—people you'c
was a ministry of presence instead of explanatio
of songs and prayers connecting with the fragmen
others, transforming a public space into a sanctu

God bless each one of you, too, and
of your days.

Notes

[1]Dietrich Bonhoeffer, *Letters and Papers fro*
enlarged ed. (New York: Macmillan, 1971), 219.
[2]Ibid., 220.

five barley loaves, left by those who had eaten, they filled twelve baskets." (Evidently, they had eaten all the fish!) John doesn't tell us what the disciples did with all those pieces of bread. Perhaps, after all these centuries, they're still being passed out, even today.

Fragments—that's all I have today, but I have been assured that fragments are something rather than nothing.

Fragment: On Tuesday someone set up a TV in "The Pit," Union's town square and meeting place. That afternoon, Jill Lum brought her daughter to school for the first time. Only four days old, the tiny girl slept soundly, completely unaware of our need to see her and touch her. Jill set the baby carrier on the table so we could gather 'round—amazed at fingernails so perfectly formed at such a young age. A wondrous miracle of life while images of death came at us from the television a few feet away. A double-exposed photograph. How can we gather up the fragments that tell us life goes on even when we fear it will not?

Fragment: Yesterday, an e-mail from my friend Viola Raheb in Bethlehem, passing on a letter from her brother Mitri. She's director of Lutheran schools on the West Bank and he's pastor of the Evangelical Christmas Lutheran Church in Bethlehem. Imagine—Palestinian Lutherans! They shared their deep sorrow and profound grief for the victims of this tragic attack. They also shared their fear and dismay: "Unfortunately, the media has shown scenes of a few Palestinians celebrating this tragedy. We want you to know that these few do not speak for or represent the entire Palestinian people." I give thanks to God that Farid Esack has come from South Africa to be with us this semester to teach "The World of Islams," to talk with us in the hallways, to read from the Koran two days ago when we gathered here raw with fear and grief. Already we have heard the news of Muslim people being attacked, of mosques and schools marred with hateful threats. What can we do as people of faith, primarily Christian, across the street from Jewish Theological Seminary, in a city increasingly Muslim? How can we gather up the fragments of understanding and hope across our different religious traditions?

Fragment: We have seen the human spirit rising amid the ashes, the unfathomable courage of ordinary people—a man carrying a woman who couldn't walk, down fifty-four stories to safety. "I only knew his name was Louie," she said. Firefighters, police, and EMTs risking their lives to save others, refusing to give up hope, searching and digging now while we worship. Long lines around the block at St. Luke's hospital on 114th Street—too many people eager to give blood. More volunteers than there are jobs. "Come back tomorrow." How can we gather up fragments of determination and courage to face together all that must be done to mend our city?

Fragment: Waking or sleeping, we cannot get the towers out of our minds—the towers that shaped the skyline and helped us find our bearings. The towers where I stood with my mom and dad from an Iowa farm, looking down in wonder at the toy buses far below, at the city spread out to the north, at the lady with the lamp in the harbor. The solid, shining towers collapsing into dust. But we knew without speaking that the towers were not empty: They were filled with people. From now on we cannot speak as we have spoken before. Never again can we use the language of "surgical strikes" or "collateral damage." From now on, we must speak of people. How can we gather up the fragments—the photos of the missing—and extend our compassion to those beyond our shores whose faces will never be posted on the walls and lampposts of our city?

Fragment: Yesterday some of you headed downtown, not knowing what to do. The blood banks were filled and the Red Cross didn't know what to do with you. So you went where people were gathering—Union Square Park. There you prayed and sang and talked with those who were searching for loved ones. Soon forty others joined you—people you'd never met. It was a ministry of presence instead of explanations. Fragments of songs and prayers connecting with the fragments brought by others, transforming a public space into a sanctuary of solace and grace. How can we at Union, with all of our own problems, be the people God is calling us to be in this city at this time?

Gathering up the fragments may be all we can do now, because any larger meaning eludes us. With God's help, we must shape meaning together in the days to come. Fragments, that's all we have. But fragments aren't nothing—excuse the grammar, but it's true! Dietrich Bonhoeffer, who once studied and worshiped in this place, talked about fragments in a letter to his friend Eberhard Bethge, written from prison in February of 1944. He acknowledged that some fragments are fit only for "the dustbin of history." But others, completed by God, come together in the manner of a fugue—the separate fragmentary notes creating something we cannot yet hear or even imagine:

> If our life is but the remotest reflection of such a fragment, if we accumulate at least for a short time, a wealth of themes and weld them into a harmony in which the great counterpoint is maintained from start to finish, we will not bemoan the fragmentariness of our life, but rather rejoice in it.[1]

I know—we aren't ready to rejoice. But it is my prayer that we will honor the fragments of hope and grief, courage and despair, and give them all to God. Bonhoeffer lifted up the fragments of his own weariness in Tegel prison: "I'm still very tired," he writes, "and unfortunately that hinders productive work considerably." You may already have discovered that this is true also for you: There is a fatigue that weighs you down even when you go to bed before midnight. Be gentle with yourself in the days ahead.

Bonhoeffer closed his letter to his friend with fragments about ordinary things:

> What is the food like? When do you get leave? When are we going to baptize your boy? When shall we be able to talk together again, for hours at a time? Good-bye, Eberhard. Keep well! God bless you. I think of you every day. Your faithful Dietrich.[2]

God bless each one of you, too, and gather up the fragments of your days.

Notes

[1]Dietrich Bonhoeffer, *Letters and Papers from Prison,* ed. Eberhard Bethge, enlarged ed. (New York: Macmillan, 1971), 219.
[2]Ibid., 220.

At This Table

Patrick Evans

Patrick Evans is associate professor of music at the University of Delaware, and artist-in-residence at Union Theological Seminary, 2001–02. This hymn text, based on John 6 and sung to the tune HOLY MANNA, was written for the service of holy communion at which Barbara Lundblad's sermon was preached—two stanzas sung prior to communion, the third stanza afterward.

At this table, feasting, praying; fruit of vine and sheaf
 of wheat;
We remember Jesus saying, "They shall have enough
 to eat."
Multitudes of weary seekers, loaves and fishes, mouths
 to feed;
"What have we among so many? We can never meet
 this need."

To this table, fragments gathered, we approach with
 anxious hearts.
Disconnected, scared and scattered, we have need to
 take our parts.
Saints from south and north surround us; words of
 care from west and east;

True communion, healing union, seeds of hope
    prepare the feast.

From this table, God of plenty, loaf remains and wine
    yet flows.
Teach us how to fill the empty, gather fragments,
    nourish souls.
Hurting people found in Jesus warm embrace in
    broken bread.
Wounded Healer, Hurt Revealer, help us feed as we
    are fed.[1]

Notes

Beautiful Feet

Heidi B. Neumark

Heidi Neumark is pastor of Transfiguration Lutheran Church, South Bronx. This was her sermon for the installation of Mark Hanson, the Presiding Bishop-Elect of the Evangelical Lutheran Church in America, held in the University of Chicago's Rockefeller Chapel on Saturday, October 6, 2001.

Isaiah 52:7–10; 2 Corinthians 4:1–7; Luke 10:1–12, 16–20

Beloved church...

What shall I preach? All flesh is grass.

"Teacher, the birds are on fire," said a kindergarten child seeing people falling in the blue sky. Earthen vessels crushed...as rescue workers sift and lift with care the pieces that remain...

What shall I preach? All flesh is grass...the grass withers, the flower fades (Isaiah 40:6–7).

, The photographs multiply like flowers around our city—smiling faces, bright eyes, identifying details springing up here and there and everywhere. He has a crescent-shaped scar on his shoulder. She has a French manicure on her hands and feet.

The papers wither and fade with hope in the rain.

The Word of God will stand forever.

But our own words...Beloved...our own words? We don't even have the alphabet.

I am grateful to whoever chose the texts for today. Isaiah, in particular, that ancient correspondent from ground zero in the sixth century B.C., has been a good companion over these past weeks.

The world-renowned city that seemed invincible, attacked and capsized by terror. Towers collapsed in rubble, bronze temple pillars broken into pieces, the glorious architectural feat and economic seat in the great city, crashed and burning.

Jerusalem 587—New York 9/11.

The sacred stones lie scattered at the head of every street, sighs Jeremiah in lamentation. Not a building, but a people: *The precious children worth their weight in gold—how they are reckoned as earthen pots...*shattered (Lamentations 4:1–2).

Jerusalem 587—New York 9/11.

Survivors in exile from all that was expected and secure. Displaced people without foothold or language, wondering where is the Word that failed to stay this chaos, as tons of paper and all the words scatter and dissolve in ash.

We don't even have the alphabet.

Jerusalem 587—New York 9/11.

A plume of bitter incense rises up from the rubble and falls again, dusting everything in sight and out of sight, sticking in our throats and lungs, and souls. You hear power generators, metal cutters, trucks, cranes...but there is nothing there that one could call a song of joy breaking forth from those ruins...and yet Isaiah tells us it will come. He too has searched through wreckage and lifted up dismembered pieces, letter by letter, phrase by phrase: *"Break forth together into singing, you ruins of Jerusalem...the* Lord *has comforted his people...The* Lord *has bared his holy arm"* (Isaiah 52:9–10a).

I've been visiting Felipe, who worked at the World Trade Center keeping the vending machines stocked with candy and chips. His wife Elba joined the via dolorosa of thousands, walking from hospital to hospital around the city, showing her picture of a proud immigrant from Honduras, a father with his arms around the two young children he adored. She held out the picture to anyone who would look, hoping against hope that she would find him alive. And then, miraculously, she did. Alive, but barely.

Alive, but covered with burns from the fiery explosion. His children wanted to see their father, but Elba shook her head, and she was right. While most of his body was hidden beneath layers of dressing, the part of his face that showed was swollen and charred, disfigured beyond recognition.

He had only the blackened remains of one ear left, but the nurses told me they believed he could hear. Later, as I lay in bed feeling sad and helpless, my husband Gregorio, also an adoring father to a son and daughter, said, "Why don't you have his children record a tape for him that will strengthen his soul?" It gave me something to do in my helplessness. Ten-year-old Leonel knew immediately what he wanted to say: "I miss you, Daddy. I wish this never had to happen. I want you to come home. I love you, Daddy." But five-year-old Rosiana was mute. I was holding a strange machine that had nothing to do with her father, who was in some strange place her mother disappeared to every morning in tears and came home from at night in anxious exhaustion. Five-year-old Rosiana had nothing to say to the gray box. Why should she? But I was unreasonably desperate to capture her voice. "Do you like to sing?" I asked, and a smile played across Rosiana's face as she nodded. I turned on the recorder and Rosiana sang to her father: "a, b, c, d, e, f, g…" I played it for a week, holding the machine close to Felipe's ear and saw no response. I also read psalms and prayed prayers, and yet I was sure that if anything would get through the fog of morphine and pain, it would be the voices of his children.

Toward the end of the second week, after grafts on his arms and chest and after much of the dead skin on his face and head and ear had been removed, I played the tape again and I saw Felipe, eyes still shut, trying to speak. I watched two words take shape on lips so fragile they bled from the effort: "Thank…you."

The words made no sound but filled the burn unit as a hymn of gratitude breaking forth from the ruins. Connection is everything. Relationship to God and to each other is life itself.

That is why we are here together today. That is why we in the ELCA are so grateful to each of you who have come from other parts of the world and from other church bodies to embody and affirm the connection we share as children of God and co-heirs with Christ. Thanks be to God and thank you! Gracias! Danke!

Permit me also to speak a word of profound gratitude on behalf of your sisters and brothers in New York. Your outpouring of love and prayer has held us up when the earth shook and the ground slipped away. The power of the communion of saints has transfused our bodies and souls with strength to go on. There is power, wonder-working power, in the blood we share!

Two weeks ago, Bishop Anderson came and visited us in New York along with President Kieschneck and President Benke of the Missouri Synod, Gil Furst and Elaine Bryant of Lutheran Disaster Relief, and all the other Regional Bishops. Their presence was the tangible expression of the larger church standing with us at Ground Zero. I think that's why Isaiah begins with the feet: "How beautiful upon the mountains are the feet of the messenger who announces peace...good news...salvation" (Isaiah 5:7).

This installation is surrounded by debate in some quarters about what we do with our hands, whose hands go on whose head. Be that as it may, Isaiah directs our attention to the feet.

Church, I think that people just might be watching the apostolic succession of our feet. Bishops...Mark, people will be watching your feet: where you walk, where you visit, where you lead, and where you allow yourself to be led.

Today we celebrate as we stand together. Recent tragedy has brought us together as a nation and a church. Yes and no. Lucia, a six-year-old girl from our church, was in McDonald's with her mother last week when another woman gave the child dirty looks, got up, and spit at her. The mother's anger flew out in her native Spanish. "¿Qué estás haciendo? ¿Estás loca?" "Oh...I didn't know

you were Spanish. I thought she was one of those…Arab people."
"Qué importa, what does it matter?" "Well, you know this is a
war." Yes, we are more united and no, we are not.

All over the city we see photos of the missing with names
and stories. Day after day they are printed in our newspapers so
that everyone can see the faces, learn the names, and mourn the
loss together, as well we should, the loss not of statistics but of
beloved individuals. In my neighborhood there are other
memorials too. Day after day, I pass them—colorful graffiti
memorials spray-painted on walls for teenagers slain on our
streets in the prime of their lives. In eighteen years, I have yet to
see a single one remembered and mourned in our city papers.
The statistics of this violence are filed away, but not the loving
details of these children whose Creator has counted every
precious hair on their heads. Yes, we are more united and no,
we are not.

Literally within minutes of becoming aware of the terrorist
attacks, people began clamoring to get to Ground Zero in New
York City—to come in person and to send all kinds of resources,
material and spiritual, for rescue, comfort, support, and the
rebuilding of life. This stampede of generosity is still going on,
and it's wonderful. You, church, have joined that marvelous
stampede. And yet…Elie Wiesel, no stranger to the geography
of terror and loss, has said that wherever human life is trampled,
wherever injustice and the suffering of human beings goes on
unchecked, there must be for us the center of the universe. In
this case it is, but more often it is not.

The daily ravages of injustice are less eye-catching than the
events of September 11, but no less devastating in their human
toll. Millions of dollars have been raised to ensure that every
family facing financial hardship or displacement due to this
terrorist attack can be helped, but what of the many more poor,
starving, sick, and homeless already? We are now moving in the
right direction to stand with the twelve-million-plus children
orphaned by AIDS in Africa and the millions more threatened
with the terror of this virus, but we could hardly claim that our

response has been a stampede of generosity. We must confess that we have dragged our feet.

People are watching our feet, church. Before coming to Chicago, I spoke with a dear brother in Christ, Father John Grange, with whom I share community organizing work in the Bronx. He spent Tuesday night at Ground Zero performing a gruesome liturgy—blessing body parts, piece after piece, all night long. He told me that he hasn't slept well since. We are naturally horrified by dismembered bodies in the rubble, but the dismembering of our human family and even the very body of Christ by racism and poverty, sexism, those who are documented and those who are not, those who are inside behind bars and those who hold the keys, and sometimes just petty matters, this gruesome dismemberment has ceased to horrify us. Many of us sleep right on through it. We have conferences and workshops, commissions and studies. We are in the city for good and it's all good, but it's not good enough. Just consider the almost crazed persistence and passion of those rescue workers carrying on without the results they hope for, insisting that there is still life to be found, lives to be restored. In the case of the firemen, they see their lost brothers as family, family they simply cannot bear to abandon. What might that tell us?

Wouldn't it be something if candidates came out of our seminaries clamoring for bishops to send them to the twin centers of the universe—North Dakota and the South Bronx? "Bishop, please I have my family to consider. That's my family there, Bishop, down those dusty roads and fields, on those tractors and in those shelters and clinics and projects, behind those prison bars, I have my children to consider, Bishop. I have the baptismal certificate to prove it! Please send me there." Or pastors in their later years, seeking a better call: "Bishop, now that I have more experience, at least to know how little I know, please consider me; please, I beg you send me to Ground Zero. I have family there." And in that vision the Board of Pensions would say: "We are one family. We have one rate, in every city, in every region. Together we'll shoulder the burden, for we are one church." And the Mission Investment Fund would jump like Jeremiah to invest in a field of rubble with prophetic passion and faith in the restoration God was sure to work. Well, church, we are united and we are not.

Mark, Isaiah also lived among a divided people: "By the rivers of Babylon—there we sat down and there we wept when we remembered Zion" (Psalm 137:1). The exiles wept as so many have wept these past weeks. "If I forget you, O Jerusalem, let my right hand wither" (v. 5). But time and distance tempered their grief and cut their sense of connection to those left behind in the inner city of Jerusalem. Interestingly for us, when the business leaders, artisans, soldiers, and priests were carried off to exile, the captain of the guard left some of the poorest people of the land to be vinedressers and tillers of the soil (2 Kings 25:12)—forsaken farmers left behind in the ruined city. So there, in what were considered the waste places of Jerusalem, you had a blend of North Dakota and the South Bronx all in one. A first-call delight!

A second and third generation in exile forgot the words and rites of their true home. Like many people today, they became willing captives to the wealth of Babylon and the lure of its new-age gods, but deep down they were as lost and disconnected as the forsaken ones back in the ruins. The rebuilding of Jerusalem was a dubious mission investment with no foreseeable return, no fringe benefits, and a lousy pension to boot. They didn't see the connection to their own renewal and life. They forgot that connection is everything; that relationship to God and to each other is life itself. And so they turned away, shaking off the dust that clung to their feet and their hearts.

And that is when Isaiah raises his voice with a blast of rhetorical force meant to rouse those exiles from business as usual to consider some other feet...some beautiful feet...feet heading straight for the waste places of Jerusalem where the arm of God is about to turn things around for everyone. "Follow those feet, folks!" shouts Isaiah. "Follow those feet!" How beautiful upon the mountains are the feet of the messenger who announces peace, good news, and salvation, who says, "Your God rules!"

Beautiful? The feet that walked upon those mountains must have been dusty, swollen, and sweaty. On the Sunday after the attack, some of our Sunday school children walked down the block to our local fire station, which lost three men when the towers collapsed. They carried cards with prayers, Bible verses, and pictures they'd made. The children saw photographs of the fallen heroes over their lockers…and in one locker, a pair of boots caked in ash, boots recovered from the rubble. "Were those his real boots?" six-year-old Derrick asked. Yes, they were. "Was he wearing them in there?" Yes, he was. "Can I touch them?" The fireman hesitated. These boots and every particle of dust they bore was precious. You could tell he didn't want that dust dislodged. "Let's just look," I said, as another fireman appeared with a plate of homemade chocolate chip cookies for the children. The dust on those boots was not the dust Jesus counseled his followers to shake off. It was dust that had something holy about it, dust that bore a message of saving love, dust from Calvary. How beautiful upon the mountains are the feet of the messenger. Beauty in those dirty boots because of where they went and why.

Isaiah directed his exiles' gaze toward the mountains where the beautiful feet appeared, with a Word that reached toward the ruins, because the prophet knew that the waste places of disconnection between the exiles and those left behind was the very space where God would gather them together and make all things new—together. Some people believe that the ELCA is heading straight to hell. Mark, please lead the stampede! (There's a line you can quote out of context!) Lead us to Ground Zero, take us to the waste places of disconnection between ourselves and others, ourselves and our God, that we too may be made new all together.

Break forth together into singing, you waste places of Jerusalem, for the Lord has comforted his people, the Lord has bared his holy arm before the eyes of all nations. The holy arm in plain sight! The Word become flesh! There it was in a dusty manger. The holy arm. Bared. So small. So vulnerable. So weak. Do you ever feel small, Mark? Powerless despite your position? Do you feel inadequate to the task? The scale of ruin at Ground Zero is beyond comprehension. It towers over the frail human forms whose tools, impressive in other contexts, appear tiny and ineffectual. There come days and times and circumstances that diminish us all. But gaze upon those holy arms bared for your sake and take heart. See how Jesus came and how he comes. He came in the very shape of your own vulnerability. We have this treasure in earthen vessels so that it may be made clear that this extraordinary power belongs to God and does not come from us. Remember that Jesus stayed and stays close to the dust, making connections with those whom others brushed aside.

"She stood behind him at his feet, weeping, and began to bathe his feet with her tears and to dry them with her hair. Then she continued kissing his feet and anointing them with the ointment" (Luke 7:38).

She ministered to him because his arm stretched out in peace had roused her from the ruins of exile where she'd been cast off by the religious establishment. "What beautiful feet," she must have thought, though surely they were rough and callused from their daily walk. "What beautiful feet because they do not shrink from me," from the gifts of ministry she brought to him regardless of whomever she did or did not sleep with. "Do you know what kind of woman it is anointing you?" they asked. He knew.

I worry about our interpretation of the gospel that tells us to wipe the dust from our feet when the Word we bear is not received as we see fit. How do we discern when to turn away from a person, a place, a people, a quota, a goal? Might we confuse the cleaning off of feet with a Pilate-like washing off of hands when attempts at mission don't seem to yield results? It puzzles me that Jesus gives this advice to the seventy when he himself appears not to have followed it.

How often have we despised and rejected the mission entrusted to us, and does Jesus shake us off? How often are we captivated by the mega-successes of Babylon, distancing ourselves from those struggling in the rubble, and does Jesus shake us off? Hardly.

They spit on him and pounded the nails into his hands and his feet. There on Calvary's Mountain—the beautiful feet, the bared arm.

According to Mark's passion narrative, it was nine o'clock in the morning when they crucified him (Mark15:25). Nine o'clock.

"Teacher, the birds are on fire"...Darkness came over the whole land. The earth shook and the rocks were split. And silence from the epicenter.

My mouth is dried up like a potsherd...You lay me in the dust of death (Psalm 22:15).

The Word itself shattered like an earthen vessel. *This is my body given for you.* Connection is everything.

On Sunday, church? On Sunday after the attack, when I came back to church with the children who'd gone down to the firehouse, youth choir practice was going on. There was Nikia, who was living with a foster family after being raped by her stepfather; Trini, who crossed the border from Mexico hidden in a truck under a pile of vegetables; Shakira, Shana, and Tyrik, orphaned when their mother died from an asthma attack while smoking crack; Donell, six feet tall and sixteen years old, who ordered girl Happy Meals on the way to Simba Camp so that his orphaned little sisters could get the toys. There was Crystal and the flock of nine siblings she shepherds to church each week where she, herself a teenager, rises above a household history fraught with abuse, homelessness, addiction, and death to teach Sunday school. They stood there on the chancel singing their hearts out.

And then it dawned on me. It was happening before my very eyes: the ruins breaking forth together into singing. Ruins? Oh no! More than conquerors, washed in our font, their names are written on the foundations of the New Jerusalem. Despite the many-headed beast that seeks to terrify and destroy, they stand before our sea of faces as conquerors beside the sea of glass with tambourines instead of harps, singing the victory song of the Lamb.

Clapping hands! Stamping feet! They rock the church! Rockin' Jerusalem! All creation stands on tiptoe, says Paul, to see all the children of God coming into their own. The trees of the fields clap their hands! The mountains skip like lambs! He stood among them and said, "Peace be with you" (John 20:19).

Peace be with you, Mark!

Peace be with you, beloved!

His feet bring joy to the scattered ruins, pulling them up with power to their feet. "You will be my witnesses in Jerusalem, in all Judea and Samaria, and to the ends of the earth…and I am with you always, to the end of the age" (Acts 1:8, Matthew 28:20).

Mark, it's simple, really. Just follow those beautiful feet!

How Can Everything Be All Right?

Alvin O. Jackson

Alvin Jackson is senior minister of National City Christian Church in Washington, D.C. This is his sermon to that congregation delivered on Sunday, September 16, 2001.

Romans 5:11

Tuesday, September 11, 2001, was a day, as President Franklin Roosevelt said of another day some sixty years ago, that will live in infamy. No longer can we tell ourselves that we are safe simply because we live in the United States. No more can we cling to the faith that our military and economic might are sufficient to protect us from our enemies. Never again can we derive comfort from our geographic remoteness, located here between these two great moats of the world. Everything changed on 9/11.

This was a wake-up call like we have never had before! Lying in the rubble that was the World Trade Center and the damaged sections of the Pentagon is the American sense of well-being. This was no less than a transforming event in our nation. Maybe for the first time in our history the entire nation has gotten in touch with the fact that we are vulnerable, and vulnerability has rarely squared with America's self-image. The notion that Americans as a people are in jeopardy fits poorly with our national sense of self and destiny. In our heads, if not in our hearts, we have known for some time that we are not immune from terrorism. The bombings of the World Trade Center in 1993 and the Alfred P. Murrah Federal Building in Oklahoma City in 1995 taught us as much. After those tragedies, parents felt compelled to reassure their children. And now this. What do we say to our children now? To ourselves? What do they say in Israel? What do they say on the West Bank and Gaza Strip? What do they say in Belfast? Certainly not "It can't happen here." Maybe just "We can only hope it won't happen here."

Our lives have been rocked. Everything that seemed so solid, sure, and secure has been shaken. And through a network of connections that unite us as families and friends and acquaintances across this country, every one of us has been affected by the devastation of that day. As John Donne said, we "never send to know for whom the bell tolls; it tolls for thee." And as Martin Luther King, Jr., often reminded us, "We are caught in an inescapable network of mutuality, tied in a single garment of destiny. Whatever affects one directly, affects all indirectly."

And so we mourn. We mourn the fatalities and the casualties, as well as our own loss of innocence. We have been attacked, and we will never feel completely safe again. And so what do we do? What do we do when the foundations of our nation and lives are shaken? One of our first impulses is to fight back, to seek out and destroy those who would seek to destroy us. If something is taken from us, we go and get it back. If we want something and it does not come, we use all available pressure to bring it about. We are a people of action. Someone once said, "When the going gets tough, the tough get going." And someone else was led to observe that, in our day and time, "If the meek are to inherit the earth, they need to become more aggressive." So when most of us face the feeling of loss, of denial, of an injustice done to us, we flex our muscles, for we want to win by persistence, ability, and tenacity. But I want to suggest another approach this morning. Maybe this is a time just to be still, at least for a moment just to be still, to reflect, to remember, to reclaim, to reconnect with each other and with our God.

And in the stillness and quietness of this moment, I want to offer a gift. Listen, if you are trying hard to believe in God while a hundred voices on the inside are telling you to stop believing, then this gift is for you. If you have prayed long and hard, but your problems, your pressures, your pain, your perplexities remain, nothing has changed, then this gift is for you. You see the evil, the suffering of the innocent, the injustice in our world, and you sometimes wonder, *Does God care?* And you ask, "How can everything be all right when everything is all wrong?" This gift is for you!

I sat the other day with family members who had lost loved ones in the Pentagon bombing. Several members of our congregation lost family members there. As I was leaving the room where family members had gathered for a briefing by members of the Pentagon staff on the recovery of their loved ones, a father who had lost a son came up to me and whispered, "Pastor, it's all right." "Yes," I said, "it's all right." But I must confess that deep in my heart, I wondered how it could be all right when everything appeared all wrong. It was all wrong for this young man's wife. It was all wrong for his children. It was all wrong for his friends. It was all wrong for his parents. And I found myself asking as I rode down the elevator to the parking garage, "How can it be all right when everything is all wrong?"

How can it be all right? We say it all the time…it's all right. A boy strikes out in a little league game and his coach says, "Son, it's all right." A guest spills coffee on a clean tablecloth and the hostess says, "It's all right." But deeper than that, not just a crying baby or spilled milk or a missed ball, but life at its depths. When you are staring death in the face, how can it be all right; when your whole world is falling apart…how can it be all right? Is it just a cliché to say it's all right? Is it profound self-deception or uncommon truth? How can it be all right when everything is all wrong?

I have been wrestling with that. I have been struggling with that question, and Paul helped me out. The apostle Paul had a saying. It was a little commonplace pleasantry, a cliché, a trivial custom, a simple platitude. For most people it didn't mean much of anything, just something you said in polite conversation. If you had been living in Paul's day, you would have heard it everywhere Greek was spoken. A man lifts a glass of wine to a stranger he meets in a bar and he might say, "Here's grace to you." Or you might sign off in a letter to a person you despise and you might say, "Grace be with you." It was just a stale, flip, silly little lie people used to oil the machinery of trivial conversation. It was just a commonplace saying, nothing more. It was like saying, "Good luck to you," "Be cool," "It's all right." Doesn't mean much of anything, just something you say.

But Paul took this little anemic, commonplace saying and rescued it and gave it a whole new meaning. Nearly every letter he wrote, he opened it with "Grace be with you," and he closed it with "Grace be with you." And here in this fifth chapter of Romans, Paul puts a theological spotlight on this word *grace* and dips it into a whole new reality. And grace becomes the signal of God's assurance that life can be all right when everything is all wrong. Grace becomes a kind of shorthand for everything God is and for everything God does in our lives. And so when you want to talk about God, about who he is and about what he has done for us, all you have to do is say *grace*. Grace makes it all right even though everything is all wrong.

And so I come this morning to offer the gift of grace. Grace, God's grace, not a cliché, not just a word without meaning, not just another theological doctrine, but the very gift of God. Not an abstract theoretical idea, not a trick or a ticket to some fantasy island, not some esoteric, ethereal notion, not some pie in the sky in the sweet bye and bye, but grace that allows us to make it in the sour now and now. Grace is that which allows us to look at earthly reality with all of its problems and pain, with all its hurts and heartbreaks, with all its sad and tragic edges and cruel cuts and still be able to say at the very center of our being, "It's all right." That's why we call it amazing grace!

I come this morning to offer the gift of God's amazing grace. This gift of grace has at least three handles, and if you can grab all three, you are on your way to real life. The first handle of grace is *pardon*. The bedrock of grace is the amazing gift of knowing that it is all right with us personally when we know that a lot of things are wrong with us. God knows that our life is not all together. God knows that we keep messing up. God knows we keep turning our backs on him. He knows our inner struggle. He sees the selfish motivation, even when we do something good. He sees the gap between our ought-ness and our is-ness. He sees that we are all vogue on the outside, but all vague on the inside. But he looks at us in all of our wretchedness and says, "I pardon you. I love you. I accept you. I forgive you. I receive you." We have been pardoned. Grace says we are pardoned.

The second handle of grace is *power*, power to lead us closer to God's image and make us better persons today than we were yesterday. But we will not sense how amazing this power is unless we see that it is unlike any energy we manipulate through our technology. Grace is a power totally unlike any we create in nuclear reactors; it is different from all physical force. But it is different, too, from moral force; grace does not make us better people by bullying us into moral improvement. The power to make us better works when God freely persuades us that it is all right with us the way we are. The power of grace is paradoxical. For the moment we know it's all right even though we are grotesquely in the wrong is the moment we are liberated from our private burdens of failure and given power to become the sort of people God wants us to be.

But not only is grace power and pardon, but grace is *promise*. The power of promise is to live now as if things are going to be all right tomorrow. Things might not be all right now, but grace is promise. Paul said, "We boast in our sufferings, knowing that suffering produces endurance, and endurance produces character, and character produces hope, and hope does not disappoint us"

(Romans 5:3–5). Grace is promise. It is the mysterious power of promise to live as if you know tomorrow will be better than today, even though common sense gives you the odds that tomorrow will be the pits.

Dr. Harry S. Wright, senior pastor of the Cornerstone Baptist Church of Brooklyn, New York, shared recently the experience of growing up in a small rural community in South Carolina. He said that his father was a hog farmer. One year when he was about nine years of age, his father had an unusually large, temperamental hog to kill. Rather than trying to handle the hog himself, his father decided to call a neighbor to help him with the hog. The neighbor came over and, with the hog locked up in the pen, took his gun, aimed, and shot the hog in the head. The hog fell down, but then got up and broke out of the pen and was headed to the open gate in the fence. Harry Wright said people started yelling, "Shoot him again, shoot him again! He's getting out! He's headed for the open gate in the fence!" But this neighbor never acknowledged the calls to shoot again and simply said, "That hog is not going anywhere, for I got off a good shot." And sure enough the hog only went a few feet and rolled over dead.

What we must know today is that on a hill called Calvary, Jesus got off a good shot, and it only looks like Satan and evil and darkness, injustice, war, racism, death, and destruction are headed for the open gate in the fence. But because Jesus got off a good shot, it is all right. Because he did, people can frustrate the will of God, but never stop it. They can slay the dreamer, but never kill the dream. They can murder the prophet, but never stop the proclamation. They can excoriate the preacher, but never exterminate the gospel. They can stone people, but never stop God. Right will win. Truth crushed to earth will rise again. God will rule. Every knee will bow. Every tongue will confess. The wicked will cease from troubling, and the weary will be at rest. Weeping endures for a night, but joy comes in the morning. Grace always has the last word!

To Mourn, Reflect, and Hope

Arthur Caliandro

Dr. Arthur Caliandro is senior minister of Marble Collegiate Church in the heart of Manhattan, New York City. This is his sermon from Sunday, September 16, 2001.

Each one of us has stories about Tuesday and what has happened since. We need to tell our stories. We need to hear each other's stories. We, ourselves, are stories.

Tuesday morning at 8:45 a.m., I got out of a taxi at the corner of Fifth Avenue and 29th Street. I heard the sound of a jet plane flying very low overhead. I looked up. I didn't see the plane, but the sound struck me as odd because one doesn't hear big jet planes flying low over Manhattan. It doesn't happen, but this day it did.

I gave it no further thought, and I went to my desk. Moments later, my younger son called me and said, "Dad, get to a television. A plane just hit the World Trade Center." As he was describing the scene, he said, "I see another plane coming. It hit the other building! What's going on? Something's happening!"

And it was. And it has.

We've seen those pictures a thousand times since. For generations of Americans, things have changed permanently.

For you and for me, things will not be the same again. America has changed forever. Something has happened.

For thirty years, as I would walk down Fifth Avenue and look straight ahead toward the very bottom tip of Manhattan Island, I would see those two gigantic buildings. And never did I see them without a feeling of awe and wonder that the human mind could create such mammoth, extraordinary structures. I never paused to calculate the immense human loss if all the people who worked in those towers ever became the victims of some attack or calamity. Even with rescue efforts underway today, we still have no way of comprehending just what the toll will be in human loss and pain.

As I look back over the years, I recall that in the first building, Tower One, there was a restaurant on the 107th floor called Windows on the World. My wife and I would often go there, bringing friends and family members from outside of the city and state. Sometimes we would enjoy special celebrations there. We would look from the south, we would look from the north, we would look from the east, we would look from the west— and see extraordinary views. We felt as if we were seeing the entire world.

Those twin towers were the symbol of American free enterprise. They were a symbol of New York and a symbol for the United States.

They were important symbols, like the Titanic. But the Titanic has sunk again and with it, thousands of lives have been lost. It's a strange feeling now, coming down Fifth Avenue and not seeing those towers there. I'm still numb. I'm stunned. Where do we look for meaning and answers when we've lost such an important symbol and when people we knew and loved are never going to return?

Time published a special edition on the attack on America, which arrived yesterday. They called those buildings "America's cathedrals." And now the cathedrals are gone. What do we do? Where do we go?

We can go to the wisdom of the ages, the scriptures, the wisdom of the universe, the word of God. In Psalm 46:5 we read:

> God is in the midst of the city; it shall not be moved;
> God will help it when the morning dawns.

God is. God has been. God will be. Nobody can destroy the city when God is in the midst of it. We depend on the presence of almighty God. We believe in it and have faith in it. It is an unchangeable, immovable presence.

What else do we do? What must we do for ourselves? Primarily, and importantly—and many people are not likely to do this, but it's essential for our mental health, the health of our communities, the health of the nation—we must take time to mourn and express our grief and our anguish. We must get deeply in touch with our feelings—the feelings of sadness, the feelings of terror, the feelings of fear, the feelings of anxiety. We need to get in touch with our anger. It is important that we get in touch with our feelings, and hold them up, and honor them. We need to respect them and give them time and space to do their work. It's important to go deep and get in touch with them.

That is why, on Friday morning, I went to see a therapist.

"Arthur, how are you?" he said. "How are you handling yourself?"

"I'm fine." I said. But I knew inside that I wasn't, and he knew that too. Then I told him how I had built a protective wall around my emotions. I had allowed none of the pain or anguish to get in. I had kept it all outside. I was protecting myself from hurt, from pain, and from feeling.

"Arthur, have you cried?" he asked me.

"No, not really," I said. "There were a couple of times when I started to, but I stopped it right away."

"Tell me about them," he said. "And as you do, cry."

I said, "I got a call from out of state, from somebody very important to me, in whom I've invested so much of myself. We had become estranged. This person had even refused to take my calls. But that person called after the disaster and when I heard that voice—'Arthur, are you all right?'—I started to cry. But I cut it off."

"Cry now," he said. And I did.

"What was the other instance?" he asked.

"This was a strange one for me," I said, "but when I heard that two of the terrorists rented a car in my hometown of Portland, Maine, drove to Boston, and came and did that dastardly thing, that got to me. There are two places that I feel that I belong, that I am passionately in love with—New York City and the coast of Maine—and both were involved, and somehow that got to me."

And I cried in his office. I learned years ago that it's one thing to cry by yourself, but it's very healing to cry in the presence of a significant other person.

"How are you feeling now?" he asked.

"I feel sad—overwhelming sadness," I answered.

He began to help me explore the sadness, and the other avenues and tributaries of my life where sadness exists. I began to discover why these two incidents got to me.

He said, "Arthur, I hope you can stay in this place of sadness." And I have. The sadness is still with me, but identifying the feeling and talking it out has relieved some pressure.

Some of you may be feeling sadness. Others of you may be feeling something different. Many of you are feeling intense anger. You're enraged. That's a legitimate feeling. Let it be, and honor it. Only share it with a thoughtful person so that it doesn't get solidified and eventually become destructive.

I have told you a part of my story. You have your story, your journey, your emotions. But please, go down deep, get in touch with the deepest feeling, and let it come out. And give it time. Give it space.

We go again to the scriptures, to the wisdom of the ages. Jesus said, "Blessed are you who mourn."

Better off are you who mourn, who grieve, who express your sense of loss, for you shall be comforted. And what he meant by that is, "You will be made whole again."

And then we know that Jesus, with a great reality check, also said, "In this world there will be tribulation, but take comfort. I have overcome the world." Then he said, "In this life you will have pain, but your pain will turn into joy."

What are we confronting when we deal with this horrific thing that has happened? We're dealing with evil. We're dealing with evil that is expressed with vicious, vicious hatred. It is anger gone mad. And when anger goes mad, when anger goes wild, it destroys.

If we were to know the personal histories of each of these terrorists, I'm certain that we would learn that somewhere in their lives, early on, they were rejected, they were hurt, they themselves were terrorized. And rather than work through the mournfulness and the grief of the emotions that hurt, they—the victims—became the victimizers.

Victims become victimizers. This is a pattern that we all know happens again and again. When something bad happens to us, we go back and inflict the pain and the hurt on somebody else.

We have to stop the cycle. We cannot institutionalize an anger that has been rigidly formed in our hearts with bitterness and vengeance.

One of our deacons, who is present today, is a top executive at American Express, whose building was across the street from the World Trade Center. When the disaster happened, she evacuated her building, left everything there, and walked up to the church. When she entered a room where a group of staff had gathered, she began to sob. Later she and I went out for a sandwich, accompanied by two members of the church's staff. As we talked, we spoke about the dark side of the human being.

Some of you remember Dr. Elizabeth Kübler-Ross, who spoke from this chancel a number of years ago. She wrote the seminal work on grief, *On Death and Dying*. In her talk, she spoke about the dark side of humanity, and gave a name to it. She said, "Each one of us has a Hitler within," which means that each one of us has within us potential for evil, for hatred and destruction.

Our deacon, that intelligent, balanced, gentle, and sensitive woman, talked with us about the feelings she was dealing with. She told us that a number of years ago, when she lived in the Midwest, her husband had been murdered in an adulterous relationship. Justice had never been served, and she said that whenever she saw someone who slightly resembled the other woman, she was angry enough to kill. Anger can do such things to us. But we must be careful with our anger and how to express it.

The other night on CNN Judith Miller, a writer for *The New York Times,* said, "We must be careful that we do not become the enemy we are fighting." I'm going to repeat that again: We must be careful that we do not become the enemy we are fighting.

We must seek justice, but not with vengeance. We go again to the scriptures, to the wisdom of the universe, to the word of God, which says: "'Vengeance is mine,' says the Lord."

Our national leaders will be planning some kind of response. Let us pray that the cycle is broken and the response is finding some way to locate these people and bring them to justice, and not to annihilate people as we have been annihilated.

Jesus spoke to just this question in one dramatic moment of his life. He was being arrested the night before He died. As the soldiers were arresting Him, Peter drew his sword and cut off the ear of one of them. And Jesus sternly said, "Enough of this, Peter. Put your sword back. Enough of this."

He was pointing to another way. And we have got to find that other way. With all of the darkness, with all of the nastiness and the horror and the sadness of this evil, we still see the greatness of the human spirit. We see extraordinary bigness. We see the wonder, we see the grandeur, we see the excitement, we see the beauty, we see the saintliness of human beings—the best of the human spirit.

The other night I was on a panel with Bill Moyers on public television. In the televised segment before our panel was on, Bill Moyers did a very poignant thing. He showed pictures of people in stress and pain. In the narrative was a litany: "We were coming down," said a man, "and they were going up. We were running out of the building. We were going for our lives, and they were going up. We were coming down, and they were going up." The ones going up were the firemen, and nearly every one of them went to his death. They responded to the call and became great.

Over the decades of time, when we have needed greatness, God has lifted up people. We have seen the greatness and the grandeur and the wonder of the human spirit here in America, in Abraham Lincoln. In India, there was Mahatma Gandhi. In England, there was Winston Churchill. In America, there was also Dr. Martin Luther King, Jr. And today in New York City, we have hundreds, if not thousands, of superheroes. They are ordinary people who, when all the others were coming down, were going up.

I have hope, I have tremendous hope.

I saw one beautiful scene reported on the news. It was tragic, but beautiful. On hearing of the tragedy, a chaplain for the New York City Fire Department changed from his clerical garb into fireman's protective clothing and went down to the disaster area. As he was giving last rites to a dying fireman, he took off his cap. In that instant he was hit by falling debris and was killed. The firemen around him picked him up, took him to the altar of a nearby church, and left him there as they went out to rescue others.

This is the beauty of the human spirit, the greatness of the human condition.

On Wednesday night, I participated in an interfaith service at Fifth Avenue Presbyterian Church, sponsored by the Partnership of Faith, a partnership of Roman Catholic, Protestant, Jewish, and Muslim clergy. There at the altar of that church, Rabbi Ronald Sobel and Shaykh Ali, both of whom have been on this chancel and have preached in this church, were speaking together in a brotherly embrace.

They represent very different backgrounds. There has been so much hostility between faith groups, and yet those two men were together. I have hope because I have witnessed the beauty and the greatness of the human spirit. We will rise again, and we will be a greater people.

Again we go to the scriptures, to the wisdom of the universe, to something that Jesus said to His disciples that we really haven't tried yet. We haven't tried it yet because we don't believe it really is going to work. But those few individuals who have tried it over the centuries know that it does work, and it makes the difference. Then, and only then, will the world be healed, when we do what we were taught to do when Jesus said to His disciples: "A new commandment I give to you, that you love one another as I have loved you."

It's a hard thing to do, but when we do it, it works. St. Paul gives us these specifics on love:

> Love is patient; love is kind; love is not envious or boastful or arrogant or rude. Love is respectful. It bears all things, believes all things, hopes all things, endures all things. There are three things in this world: faith, hope, and love. Faith is important. Hope is essential. But the greatest of them is love. (1 Corinthians 13:4–6, 13, alt.)

Let us pray.

Our Father God, be with us in our grief. Help us to be in touch with the feelings. Help us to work through the feelings that we might be comforted. And, Lord God, please, please help us to love. Amen.

The Familyhood of Humanity

James A. Forbes, Jr.

The Rev. Dr. James A. Forbes, Jr., is senior pastor of the interdenominational Riverside Church in New York City. This sermon was preached there on Sunday, October 7, 2001.

Luke 10:25–37

I noticed as I listened to some of my sermons that I usually begin by saying, "Brothers and sisters." There may be a reason why that is the most common expression I use when addressing a congregation of worshipers. I think that's one of the highest kinds of titles to apply. Oh, yes, "friends"—that's good. But brothers and sisters, I greet you today with a special sense of the meaning, "brothers and sisters."

> Holy Spirit, lead me, guide me as I move
>   throughout the day.
> May your prompting deep inside me show me
>   what to do and say.
> In the power of your presence, strength and
>   courage will increase.
> In the wisdom of your guidance is the path that
>   leads to peace.
> *Thank you. Thank you.*

This prayer was prompted by my realization that after September 11, I was experiencing many different feelings, and discovering conflict between my first and second opinion. Listening to the various views presented on the news—reactions sometimes positive, sometimes negative. Engaging in the waving of the flag at Yankee Stadium with a sense of solidarity with my nation and yet, aware of the use of the flag not only as an expression of patriotism but for some even sheer protection against the scowls on the faces of others—almost as if to say, hey, I am an American, too. Listening to the proposals regarding what we must do in retaliation and retribution, fully confident that I appreciate the security that I enjoy as an American citizen, not unmindful that military peacekeeping helps to sustain something of the security we have come to enjoy. And, yet, at the same time not so sure about characterizations of us as the good guys and everybody else as the bad guys. Feeling deeply about the assault against us. Feeling that there must be justice, that we cannot in this world allow that kind of behavior to go unchecked. We must do something to stop it. At the same time hoping that we don't think that simply by some swift military action we will blot out for now and all eternity every manifestation of terrorism. Appreciative for the restraint that I see, uncertain about what will finally be unleashed.

Am I the only person swinging from one of these sides to the other, wondering just how Christ would have me respond? So it was out of that swinging, that vacillation, that I thought it's not even safe to leave my house without asking for the assistance of the Holy Spirit. So that's where these words came from.

Holy Spirit, lead me, guide me as I move
   throughout the day.
May your prompting deep inside me show me
   what to do and say.
In the power of your presence, strength and
   courage will increase.

In the wisdom of your guidance is the path that
   leads to peace.

In this spirit everything now gets reviewed in the light of what I consider a more contemporary spiritual meaning. For example, every scripture I have read since September 11 has taken on slightly different meanings. Take the parable of the good Samaritan. It's not the same parable for me that it was before September 11. Let me tell you why. The lawyer who stands up to test Jesus asks, "What must I do to inherit eternal life?" This is a question that I see differently now. Is that what we seek? What are we really looking for? Are we looking for a life of comfort? Are we looking for life free from tyranny? Are we looking for life on this side of the river Jordan? Are we looking for life on this side and the other side? There's a difference, you know that for people for whom life as we know it on this side is the primary concern, then secure me now is the attitude of the day. Protect me now. Do whatever you have to do to allow me a few more golden moments. I deserve to live. I must live. Do whatever you want to do to diminish that which would tend to threaten my longevity in life. I want life not only with security but I want it with comfort. Whatever it takes to secure the comforts I have grown accustomed to. Do that.

Well, now that I'm reading about this lawyer, here in the tenth chapter of Luke, I assume that whatever eternal life means, it means life touched by the values we have learned in our faith. It means life that God will grant both in time and in eternity. It means life lived so that I can look at myself in the mirror and answer that question, "Have you done anything to diminish the life quality of anybody else?" So that I can look in the mirror or into the face of God and say, "I have already started my eternal life." I live by eternal principles so that I will be able to end with a sense that I did what I had to do, and if there is a St. Peter and St. Peter is standing at the gate, and they've got the book up there, and they run their fingers down until they get to FORBES, then he thumbs over to look at my profile. To live eternal life is to have comported with the values that I wish to stand by.

Well, I look at that differently. I'm asking questions, What am I living for? What does eternal life look like? Would I ever sacrifice some of the comforts and even securities in this life to stand me in better stead in the life to come? These are questions that now I don't just pass over. I find myself wondering about these things. But then you know how Jesus answered him. He says, well, what's in the law? What would your background lead you to think would be the path that so conforms to the will of God that, if there is a reservation you need at the hotel in the New Jerusalem, you'd get it? And he answers the question. "You've got to love the Lord your God with all your heart, all your mind and all your soul and all your strength and your neighbor as yourself." Jesus answered, "You have answered right. If you do that, you will live."

That's a pretty good example of the quality of life we are called upon to live. That is, to love the Lord our God with all our hearts, all our mind, all our soul, all our strength. That's a pretty good journey right there. And then love our neighbor as our self. That's tough, especially right through here. Suppose that neighbor looks like an Arab or worships at the mosque or looks like some of the pictures we have seen of the terrorists or has association with things we consider to be sort of Middle Eastern. All of a sudden it's getting harder and harder to be confident when I stand before the throne of God. Oh, may I be candid with you? There have been reports about people who have been killed because they look like the terrorists. It has happened on college campuses that students have become vigilantes against folks that look different. One of my friends said that she went to a movie and she happened to sit down beside someone who looked to her like some of the pictures that she had seen, and she said she did not enjoy the movie. For some strange reason, that person kept looking at his watch throughout the movie. She doesn't know how the movie ended. She left early.

That brings up profiling. Surely, there has got to be some logic to paying closer attention to those pictures you have seen, but I want to ask a question here this morning. Do you know that for everybody in here somewhere in the world there are people who have suspicions about people that look like you? Because everybody who is a part of any kind of extended family will have somebody in that family who from time to time will do things that are worthy of our suspicions, worthy of our judgment, worthy of justice. Just think of it. I know about that. Two friends, one black and one white. Buddies, chums, racing to get to the bus. As the bus is coming the one who is black is running faster and the one who is white is a little bit behind him, and as they get to the bus, the cop stops the black one— assuming that the black one has stolen the purse of the white one who is running behind him. Only to be told, no. We are buddies. We're both running trying to catch the bus.

Do you hear what I'm trying to say? There is a reality that we, on the basis of similarity of appearance, will from time to time think, surely that's the one. Oh, there are some folks who are afraid of black folks. But you need to know that there are some folks who are afraid of white folks. And you need to know that there are folks who are afraid of Christians. And there are places in the world where folks are afraid of Protestants, places where folks are afraid of, well, whatever your tradition. What kind of world will it be if everybody is typecast according to the less civil members of the group to which we belong? What would have it been like if, after they were mistaken for a couple of days in the Oklahoma City bombing looking for Arabs, and, lo and behold, it was McVeigh. What kind of world would it be like if we all got ready to sniff out who it is we should be afraid of, whom we should arrest, whom we should suspect, whom we should be willing to kill, no matter what. Oh, all I'm really telling you is why all of a sudden texts don't mean exactly what they used to mean to me, for when Jesus tells this brother, "You have answered right," and he asks, "Well, who is my neighbor?"—all of a sudden I'm cast back into our time and then I go back to that time.

You know the story. It won't take long to tell it again. Jesus says, who is your neighbor? The text says that this brother asked that question seeking to justify himself. Is there anybody here today who does not need justification? Is there anybody here who is not like this lawyer? I have to be kind to my lawyers. They work hard to help keep things moving around here. But isn't it true that from time to time somebody you think is going to be mean to you turns out to be an agent of love and care to you and you almost are surprised? May I be candid? In my past in the South they used to tell me, "Jim, we like you because you are a good Negro." And I didn't have the heart to say, and we like you because we think you are a good white person. And we don't mind our corner grocer because he's a good Jew. And we have Muslims who are good Muslims. This corrected adjective before groups of people I call "ethnic exceptionalism." We've already characterized the particular group as bad, but in our Christian charity we will select some out of that bad crowd that will be all right.

That's how the story of the Good Samaritan got its name. Everybody knew that the Samaritans were bad folks. Everybody listening to Jesus knew it. And the disciples knew it. They had tried to pass through a Samaritan town and they would not even let them overnight there. And James and John said, Lord, do you want us to call down fire and burn up these Samaritans, these half-breeds, these people who were collaborators with our enemies, these folks that have got the nerve to put up some other place than Jerusalem? We need to keep them out. Look at how they dress. Look at how they eat. These awful Samaritans. Everybody that heard Jesus tell the story knew that the Samaritans were the terrorists of the day. In fact, some said, people even prayed, "Lord do not be merciful to them lest their growth further contaminate the earth."

So, back to the story. A man going out from Jerusalem to Jericho fell among robbers and thieves who took him and beat him and stripped him of his clothes, leaving him half-dead. What ethnic group do you think the robbers were from? Oh, exegesis would say they might have been Arabs or they might have been Samaritans, which throws altogether new light on the story, doesn't it? I mean, first of all, the reason that the priest sees the man half dead and passes by is because the priest, if he's going to do his duty, cannot be contaminated with anybody dead, so clearly if he looks like he's dead, then the priest is going to walk, so he can do his duty under God. And next I'd like—this is not biblical, this is just sanctified imagination—I'd like to think that the Levite who was passing by showed at least some human concern, so he goes over and he stops—but then he swiftly moves on. I think I know why. See, in my way of looking at the story, he saw this Samaritan way down. On those open spaces you can see no trees. It's desert area now as you're going down. He saw somebody whose headgear and attire looked like it might be one of those blankety, blank, blank, blank, blank Samaritans. And everybody knew how the game was played. Sometimes the way robbers did it, is they allowed one to look like he needs help and somebody comes along to help and then they all spring out and they take you, too. You all get what I'm trying to say to you. This brother could see, and he thought the brother is only half-dead. So he goes on.

And what a story Jesus tells. And you can see the people who are listening begin to sense that this story is a trick story. It is dealing with the way we profile. It is dealing with the way we respond to people on the basis of external conditions. And so Jesus says, although the two pass by, along came a Samaritan. And this Samaritan stopped, saw him half dead, and drew near unto him, took out his oil and his wine, mixed it as household remedies are, and applied it to his wounds, and had enough cloth to bandage up his wounds. And then picked him up, put him on his own beast of burden, took him to an inn, stayed overnight to make sure he'd make it through the night, or at least this may have been his stopping-off place. I mean, folks knew him. And here presumably the poor man who has been robbed is a Jew. But here is this Samaritan taking him probably to the inn that Samaritans were allowed to use and even risking questions, what are you doing with this Jew in here, this is a Samaritan stopping-off place? Stayed overnight, took off the next morning and gave two denarii, saying, "You take care of him, and if there is any further cost that you incur you wait until I return and I will reimburse you."

Then Jesus turns the question, "Which one of these three do you think was the neighbor to this man?" And his answer, the obvious, the one who showed mercy to him. He was the neighbor. So Jesus had shifted from "Who is my neighbor?" to "What is neighborliness?" because you're going to need to love God but also love your neighbors. And Jesus says, you go and do likewise.

Exegesis tells us that we have to make sure who we identify with to get the full benefit of this parable. Do we identify with the priest, who must for ritual reasons keep himself clean? Do we identify with the Levite, who did have concern but not yet born into compassion? Or do we identify with the poor victim, who is being looked at and who is the object of scorn? Who do you identify with? And no matter which one of those three you identify with, you identify with the innkeeper for at least trusting the Samaritan to come back. The text suggests that maybe this is Jesus' autobiography. One who has come from homeplace. Jesus, who has come from our hometown and finds us wounded, assaulted, attacked. And Jesus gets down and through his ministry puts on the balm of Gilead—Jesus, who is not afraid to risk his life to ensure that everybody that came from the hometown is taken care of, and not only ministers individually, but institutes a system of care.

That's Jesus, and because I'm a Christian I'm called to identify with him. And what is the hometown? The hometown is heaven. Jesus is from my hometown. And guess what? Everybody else on the face of the Earth is from the same hometown if you get right back to it. Therefore, Jesus seems to be suggesting in this story that the world that gives us access to eternal life is a world we build in which we assume everybody we see is not only from the hometown but, like in South Carolina, we're all relatives of one another. That's why I call you brothers and sisters every morning when I get up here. Oh, we're the same. Some of you look the way you do, and some of you look the way I do, and then there are variations. But guess what? We're all brothers and sisters.

And as we come to this Columbus Day weekend I'm thinking about the wisdom of our Native Americans, who tell us that we all are members of one Earth. We are all members of a network interwoven; the fabric of humanity is of one web, and anybody who destroys one thread in the fabric is also destroying himself or herself.

Well, I close this morning with this. This morning we're going to have communion by intinction, and that means that people who are to be served today have to get up. They've got to get up. I'm coming now to the table, but let me explain what the problem is. If there's anybody for whom walking down to the front is maybe a threat, we've got to make sure that that doesn't happen here today. You see, churches have to be places that are different from the world. There must be a place where if somebody felt that I look like a terrorist and my name sounds like a terrorist I can go where I don't have to be afraid, where I can walk down if I want to take the communion or either walk down just to pass by if my religious tradition does not allow me to do so. We've got to make this place safe in here. And one of the ways we're going to make it safe is to say to you we are not alone. People care for us who are not even here. These aisles here hold cards that we have received from around this country. From people…they say, to your church family. This is from St. Louis, Missouri. This is from Saskatchewan, Canada. When you walk around I want you to stop and receive greetings from people who care about us. They don't look like us. They may be different nationalities, but on worldwide communion Sunday they know we are one.

So today if I had a Muslim brother I'd tell him I know one place that's safe for you. Come to Riverside Church. Or my Jewish mother here. I'd tell her you are safe here and you don't have to hide either in the balcony or down in the back. It's a place where you can walk around, because we want to get to heaven, and we can't get there until we learn how to build a world where we need not fear the robbers on the road nor the innkeepers who keep the shops nor the priests nor the Levites.

We want a world where people can be free, and we can't get to that place without some risk. It's going to be some risk to try to build that kind of world. We are compartmentalized, broken up, and anybody who tries to work for peace may even be considered unpatriotic, but we are called upon to be one world where we are one family.

That's why I invented the word, I guess, the "familyhood" of all humanity. It's not in the dictionary, because that's not even the way we think, but the truth be known, Jesus is from the hometown, and the truth be known, he says, we're all kinfolk. Don't let the externals fool you—we have come made from one blood. And if that's not enough, then those of us from the Abrahamic faith need to understand that the only reason any one of us can think of ourselves as chosen is because through us all the families of the earth shall be blessed. This is why, here's what I ask you to do, this morning we're going to invite you to pass the peace. But as you pass the peace I want you to hold the hands of the person long enough to find out what their name is and where they're from. This is worldwide communion Sunday. And when they tell you where they are from, tell them you are safe in the family of God. Fear not. We will do what we can to make this world the kind of place where you need not fear for your life, and after that we then begin to get ready to come to the table, and everybody is welcome. If you are not a Christian, when they come, you come around, and you don't have to take communion—just come around and just march on back to your seat, for this is the kind of world we are praying that God will help us to build through the power of love. It's peacetime. Don't make it quick. Let us stand and pass the peace to one another. Let's take time.

Always Looking for the Lost

Suzanne Webb

Suzanne Webb is interim senior pastor of Park Avenue Christian Church in Manhattan, New York City. This sermon was preached there on Sunday, September 16, 2001.

The preacher's responsibility is to proclaim and interpret the Word of God into the midst of daily life.

A service of worship offers a sanctuary—not just an architectural wonder, but sacred emotional space—where the encounter between God and each person may occur. The intention of sacred space is to provide safety for the very most vulnerable moments of our lives—and yet, essentially to do it publicly, because there are others in the space.

One of the women who walked into this sanctuary on Wednesday had never really noticed this building before, but had just come from taking care of pets of her friend—who had not returned from a Tuesday morning meeting at Windows on the World. The woman sat in this space, was with us through a prayer service—then broke down, claiming she had been *strong* until she came into the church. She may never return to this sanctuary—but for that hour, that day, the facade of strength that she had built around herself in order to cope had been allowed to be penetrated.

Friday night this holy space was filled to overflowing with people—most of whom we do not know—but all of whom needed a sanctuary where their lives could intersect with an articulated presence of God.

So we gather this morning, in a space known for allowing our vulnerabilities to be exposed, now searching for and waiting to hear some word or *The Word* from God. Once we walk through those doors, the space, the music, the words of scripture, the people gathered, the taste of bread and wine, and yes, the word proclaimed all have the potential of breaking through to the interior heart and soul of each person here. Therefore, what is said can have a very, very serious impact.

Some of the other words we have heard already this week:

We will avenge this atrocity. America didn't choose the beginning, but we will choose the ending of this war.

New Yorkers are resilient and now need to get back to normal—to work, to eat out, and shop.

And, most recently: This is God's message to our own self-inflicted corruption.

Those are three centers of rhetoric that are drawing people like magnets in this city, this country, and this world. Dear brothers and sisters, there is another word that emerges, and one that we must write and speak together with God. It will take our lifetime. It will take our life's ambition. It will take our life's energy. But it is one that we are called to—even more poignantly this day than a week ago.

The gospel of Jesus Christ, which we heard today read from Luke, has as a major theme that God is always looking for that which is lost. The question is, Have we lost the gospel?

Looking for the lost is an all-consuming activity—as we have seen with the thousands working downtown around the clock since Tuesday. But looking for the lost gospel is more than looking for bodies or evidence. What God is looking for—and begs for us to be looking for as well—is that part of our human soul that would see a face on every living human being created, a face loved and created by God. For our own protection, we have found ways to dismiss that reality, to lose it, and so our societies have been able to depersonalize enemies and, therefore, justify their destruction. We must—as a faith community—figure out ways to find, reclaim, and teach the gospel, to reweave it into our psyches and the social fabric of our world.

Is there one of us who has not seen a movie or a TV show in which an enemy has been put down and we have cheered, either audibly or in our heart? To us, one of the most appalling sights this week was the dancing in the streets in the Middle East when news of the hit on America came. That anyone would/could cheer at the destruction of our city was an awakening. It is not the buildings *we* mourn—though certainly they were symbols of strength—but it is the lives and faces of real people, people *we* know, people who lived in our buildings, who walked in our neighborhoods, who worked in our businesses. But *our* faces were not known to those dancers. They were cheering and celebrating as we have become accustomed to when we watch movies and the enemy camp has been blown up.

When I moved to Switzerland several years ago into an international community, I was on dishwashing duty the first day. In keeping with my bubbly persona, I thrust out my hand to my dishwashing buddy. "Hi, I'm Suzanne from the United States." And he said, "Hi, I'm Jean from the Sudan."

That moment is still frozen for me. Here was a face and hand of the people that my country had just bombed, killing scores of non-military citizens. Even though I had not cheered when that had happened, I never anticipated having to live with someone of that heritage.

What we have lost, and must look for until we find it, are ways to teach our children—so they may teach their children—that it is possible to resist violence, that there have to be ways to stop evil that do not merely escalate it.

The church and other faith communities are going to make the difference, or the difference will not be made. We are the ones who have the legitimate claim to that message. And unless we take hold of that, sweep until we find it, we might as well be clanging symbols, empty vessels, and worn-out museum pieces.

As we search for and teach this faith that every person has a beloved face, we are also aware that profiling has reared its ugly head once more. Here again, the gospel—if we find its true message—will not tolerate such activities. If this isn't *the* most open and affirming city in the world, it is close to it—which, of course, coincides with the ministry of diversity of this congregation. A strike of terrorism like Tuesday's threatens that diversity. Our response can do so as well. Stereotyping a face also denies that real and beloved person within a body.

The most devastating "religious" statement we have heard is that God allowed this destruction because God was weary of our allowing and condoning diversity. God created diversity! I believe God is weary because we minimize that reality. God must be worn out when we cannot see all others as anything but members of the same family.

We have got to keep searching. We have got to keep sweeping. We have got to keep working until we find the message of God that seems to be lost in all of the chaos of our present life.

That message and that search has to do with building a world with God that will not allow for differences to turn to hatred, and hatred to turn to violence, and violence to be thrilling— and the thrill to be celebrated because we can remove the faces of those we are hurting.

There is one family on this earth—and it does not live under one flag.

Yes, we are a resilient people—as New Yorkers, and as Americans—and that is something of which we can be proud, and we must celebrate and encourage it. But even more importantly, we have to seek the faithful and courageous way to proclaim the gospel of Jesus Christ that builds an appreciation for each child of God as a part of God's family.

God has not abandoned us and never will. God has not orchestrateed the destruction of this city or its people and never would. But God is calling us even in the midst of this time to find ways to re-form the fabric of our lives so that we will be able to stand against evil and not become a part of its perpetuation.

Scientifically, we have amazing contributions to claim—even within the last fifty years—of space travel, telecommunications, cloning animals. And what are our contributions of faith in these years? We have a lot of work to do, people of faith. We also have amazing contributions to make—that have to be made or the violence will continue. It will be claimed to be justified, and human arrogance will grow to an overwhelming level.

This is the moment of possibility for lives to be changed, the moment to be on the search for the message of God in this world, for sweeping away the debris, and claiming what God would have us do and be.

We come into this holy space today for comfort, but also for strength. We have the gospel to find. We have the gospel to proclaim. We have work to do—with God—to help change the very fabric of our lives, and the life of humanity.

A Meditation of the Heart

William A. Greenlaw

The Rev. Dr. William A. Greenlaw is rector of The Church of the Holy Apostles in New York City—a congregation where the homeless are fed in the sanctuary as an act of eucharistic fellowship. This sermon was preached there on Sunday, September 23, 2001.

May the words of my mouth, and the meditations of our hearts be always acceptable in your sight, O Lord, our strength and our redeemer. Amen.

How often have you heard those or similar opening words to a sermon from any of the clergy here, and heard them as a mere verbal formulary—a time to clear the throat, get comfortable, to get settled in for whatever it is that is to come? I will confess that sometimes those words seem completely formulaic. But I am particularly struck by them this morning.

I don't know when I have ever felt such uncertainty, such hesitancy, such unclarity in preaching, as I have felt in preparing a sermon for this morning. I have had more false starts than I care to think about, even a full draft good only for the circular file. In short, I really am not sure about those "words of my mouth" this morning.

The "meditations of our hearts"? Well, I know I am not alone in feeling an overwhelming sense of distraction, of fear, of anxiety, of uncertainty. Of being frightened by some of the thoughts I have had in my sense of being violated by something quite literally "out of the blue." Meditation? That has been hard this week.

How can we imagine that either my words or the individual and collective hearts of those gathered here this morning could possibly be described as "acceptable," much less "always acceptable"?

But at a very late hour, it finally came to me. I found I could continue, inadequately as it may feel to me or seem to you. And that is simply because my words are offered and our hearts are known and accepted by a Lord who is indeed both our "strength" and our "redeemer"—even in, especially in, times like these.

And if we here can connect on some level with that One who is our Source, our Life, our All—then for what more could we ask? For Christ meets us precisely in our weakness and fear and uncertainty with a redemptive power that alone can redeem and make whole—even when we can barely get a fix on where we are, on what has happened to us, on where we might be going.

Our Collect of the Day also is far too often for us a sort of pious, formulaic ditty that means we can finally anticipate getting to sit down after the Processional Hymn, Opening Acclamation, Collect for Purity, and Gloria. But there are often gems of theological insight in the petitions that are made. "Grant us, Lord, not to be anxious about earthly things." Hey, that's hard. We're Anglican Incarnationalists, after all. Creation is good. No, it's "very good." God sent Jesus to transform our lives here, not just to prepare us for whatever may come next. Don't be anxious? When we know perhaps with more clarity now than ever before about being "placed among those things that are passing away"— broadcast over and over on CNN in case we missed it with our very own eyes?

How do we, how can we, do we even want to "love things heavenly" and "hold fast to those that shall endure"—whatever those pious phrases might mean while in the midst of such devastation and uncertainty? On more than one occasion this past week, I thought I would rather scream—or lash out at just anything or anyone that gets in my way.

But what finally came to me is simply this. In my own, and in our shared, impotence, about the only sure thing we can do is to pray, to be willing to open ourselves in our weakness and vulnerability to the God who loves us even so, who has not abandoned us.

We can pray for strength, for guidance, for understanding. We can pray for the wisdom of discernment and restraint. We can also pray for the strength to act on the faith that is within us.

Having shared with you a bit of my own convoluted journey this past week, let me share with you some very preliminary reflections on our current situation.

Most of us were simply repulsed by the words of Jerry Falwell and the endorsement of them by Pat Robertson, in suggesting that the terrorist attacks were brought on by the ACLU, feminists, gays, and lesbians—all of them nefarious forces of evil that incurred God's wrath. Enough flak resulted that Falwell was forced to retract his statement, and thank God he did.

But what do we do with Amos? Amos, like so many of the prophets of ancient Israel, discerned rampant injustice in the land—while the official political and ecclesiastical establishment proclaimed that God's blessing was sure. But Amos was clear that a land that would "trample on the needy, and bring to ruin the poor of the land" would, ultimately, be brought to judgment.

Now, when I first looked over this lesson from Amos in the context of our situation today, my first inclination was to set it aside, for a people who are reeling from terror need comfort and reassurance and a sense of God's loving presence before they need this. And besides, weren't we the ones who were violated by terrorists? What has this got to do with us, anyway?

Well, perhaps, just this. Why is it, how is it, that so many in this world revile us, would seek to do us such harm? We so often see ourselves as the bastion of both freedom and free enterprise, of incarnating a virtue and sense of destiny that is simply unknown in human history. We are the envy of the world. People from all over the world seek to come here.

But such cultural imperialism neatly sidesteps that our standard of living, our mindless, unconscious consumption of so much of the world's resources, our arrogance, our indifference to the world's environment, standing almost alone in the community of nations, our continued support of repressive regimes perhaps now especially in the Islamic world—all these things provoke not only disdain but rage in the hearts of more than a few.

And the horrible irony is that in our efforts to stop the Soviets in Afghanistan in the early 1980s, we sided with the most extreme elements there and in Pakistan—and those destabilizing elements have become the Taliban and supporters of Osama bin Laden. But let it be noted, as the Soviet Union and its empire was crumbling in all the world, it was also stopped dead in its tracks in Afghanistan.

How does this relate to Amos? Only that human blindness individually and collectively has always been, and remains the greatest among those who are in power, who find ways of justifying and explaining their policies and proclaiming their virtue and favor by God—all the while either practicing or condoning the most egregious injustices.

If history tells us anything, such blindness contains the seeds of its own destruction within it. This is how God's judgment seems to work itself out in history.

Is it possible that in our need to respond to the real evil of terrorism, we might also ask some basic questions about how and why we are perceived by much of the rest of the world, and about why there are people who embrace such a fanatical hatred of us?

Is it possible that in our need to respond to the real evil of terrorism, we might refrain from actions that can only create more hatred toward us—and therefore actually further the terrorist's own agenda? B52s are, by their very nature, indiscriminate in the damage and carnage they inflict. Is this how we fight terrorist cells? How far do we expect the rest of the world to follow us in our need to act decisively—but against whom? For what?

There is at most a two- to three-week food supply for those parts of Afghanistan that have any food at all. Many places have none. Starvation was already widespread. Countless refugees are trying to flee, but borders are closed, and there is no refuge, no food. The Afghani people have suffered for so long in war under an impossibly repressive regime, at least in part, of our own making. What is happening to them even now before a shot, so far as we know, has even been fired? Can we begin to imagine their suffering even now? Who will be there for them when hostilities break out? Do we even care?

Where else is our "war" going to take us? Who is our "enemy"? Just how are we going to fight them? How much "collateral damage"—newspeak for innocent, civilian casualties—are we willing to inflict? And, as a consequence, how much new hatred and instability are we going to create? Where will it all end?

Might it be possible that religious people and others could make their voices heard in this perilous time?

I admit that, at heart, I am an old-fashioned product of the 1960s—an era when we thought and believed we could make a difference, whether it be through the civil rights movement or in opposition to the war in Vietnam. There was a lot of headiness, a lot of hubris, a lot of unrealism back then. We also know that since then, cynicism has been more the norm. And yet, who would have imagined that "the movement," as it used to be called, could have emerged out of the Eisenhower era of the 1950s? And yet it did.

Out of very real tragedy could there be a reawakening of concern in our land about the most basic issues of social justice and peace? The Internet is ablaze with statements, petitions, news of religious and other groups everywhere over these questions. Even through the heated rhetoric of Washington, and dare I say it, even in our president, I have seen at least some signs of sensitivity, awareness, and restraint. Of our president visiting an Islamic center in his stocking feet. Of our not tolerating discrimination against Muslims. Of making clear our "enemies" are not Muslim nations filled with innocent people. That gives me a bit of hope, a bit of some sense that maybe we don't have to be on a new crusade that will take us to every corner of the world. But then we need to make our voices heard and hold our leaders accountable to their own words.

Dear Friends, what a time this has been. I have found myself slowly moving a bit beyond the immediate shock and grief and disbelief over the events of September 11. Yet still, every time I take our dog out the back door and pass by the station house of Rescue 1 of the Fire Department of New York, tears come—I simply cannot hold them back. I see amid the flowers and candles and drawings the pictures of an entire shift that was lost, and I recognize them all, and I see the incredible response of my neighbors. And suddenly, once again, there are no words to express the wonder and awe and gratitude I feel toward those firefighters whom I took for granted for so long. And there is a new sense of community present.

There are no adequate words to speak in being with those who have lost loved ones in the World Trade Center attack. No words at all. Just a caring presence. Just a grieving community. Just taking one step, one day at a time. Of holding—and being held.

The final thought I would leave with you is simply this. If we can take the grief, the loss, the devastation we feel over these events—and just try to take in that every time a life is lost through war or terrorism anywhere in the world, there are people, real people like you and me, who are also living through singular grief and loss and devastation—then just maybe we can find the strength to work to ensure that we do not create still more death and destruction in an already suffering world, as our nation seeks to rid the world of terrorism.

I close with a prayer adapted from the Archbishop of Canterbury.

O God, your son Jesus Christ taught us to have trust in you; we pray that, out of this darkness the light of Christ may shine; that out of this pain may come healing; and out of this destruction may come new life and hope. Deliver us, we pray, from hatred and malice, from fear and mistrust. Bless the President of the United States, his advisers, and all the people of America, united in grief and undivided in their sorrow, that working together for your purposes, the darkness of this present time may be turned into the dawn of new life, through our savior, Jesus Christ. Amen.

What Is Broken, Matters

Bonnie Rosborough

The Rev. Dr. Bonnie Rosborough is pastor of Broadway United Church of Christ in New York City, where she preached this sermon on Sunday, September 16, 2001.

Exodus 32:7–14; Luke 15:1–10

On the occasion of retiring as president of Bangor Theological Seminary, United Church of Christ leader Ansley Coe Throckmorton shared a story appropriate for our worship today. It seems one December a group of parents waiting to collect their small children for Christmas vacation stood outside a classroom in which their children had been working for some time to make ceramic gifts for their families' holiday trees. As the children were released that afternoon they ran down the hall excitedly, proudly carrying their brightly wrapped packages with them. One small boy trying to run, pull on his coat, and wave to his mother at the same time tripped and fell. The surprise flew from his grasp and shattered in pieces on the tile floor before him. After a moment of stunned silence, the child began to wail his disappointment and loss. An adult, trying to comfort the boy by minimizing the incident, patted his arm and murmured, "There, there it doesn't matter." But the child's mother knew

74

better. She rushed up, dropped to her knees alongside her boy, and swept him into her arms. "Oh, but it does matter," she said compassionately. "It matters a very great deal indeed!" And that mother wept with her distressed child.

My brothers and sisters, if in these last few days you have searched for an image of the Almighty that could help you make sense of the suffering that's come upon us; or if you have heard the question, as I have, "Where, oh where, is God?" then I say, "Look to that mother," for it is in her that we see reflected the image of a God who weeps with the knowledge that *what is broken matters.* It matters very much indeed; and it is in this God, whom we know in Jesus Christ, falling where we have crumpled and sweeping our bloodied lives into his body, that we have hope.

The British philosopher Alfred North Whitehead once described God as "The Tender Care That Nothing Be Lost," and this is the Sovereign One we're talking about today: The Tender Care That Nothing Be Lost. Moreover, I believe it is with this understanding of God that our texts for this fifteenth Sunday after Pentecost are concerned.

The story from Exodus is familiar, and in many ways it is disturbing, because God is portrayed here as being so angry. Moses has been up the mountain. While he is away the Hebrews have gone astray—fashioned the Golden Calf. Yahweh is furious because, as we know, these are God's people (chosen, redeemed, covenanted, loved), and isn't it always true that it is those whom we love who hurt and anger us most? Well, the Lord God of Exodus, this anthropomorphic deity we know from the Pentateuch, is not exempt from these feelings. Yes, in power the Almighty had split the Red Sea wide open, but this power doesn't exempt God from being vulnerable nor does it insulate God from hurting. And it is the hurt that is portrayed in the verse we've just heard read. God is hurt because God's people who matter have turned away and been lost. Hurting so, the God of Exodus wants to strike out, just as you and I might; but, mercifully, Moses intercedes. God relents.

Yet as we too well know, the human tendency to go astray tragically persists—which, generations later, is precisely the reason for Jesus, whose mission it was to rescue the broken and lost. "I came for the sinners, not the righteous," he says, telling two parables about the extreme measures one in God's realm goes to in recovering the lost sheep and the lost coin, thus emphasizing the point: The lost matter, the hurt matter—disproportionately, unreasonably, eternally—we matter.

God cares. This is why God's was the very first heart to break Tuesday morning when this great suffering came upon us. God did not remain remote on Tuesday nor has God shouted counsel from a safe distance since then. God was there. God is there, catching that which tumbled down.

God is present. God is pained. And God is powerfully mad.

If Jerry Falwell and Pat Robertson and their like think God is angry and hurt, they're right, but it is not because this nation has turned to abortion, homosexuality, or the ACLU, as they've suggested. God's anger is in direct proportion to God's love, and it is fiercely stirred now—not in retaliation but in consolation—for God's children are harmed. Don't let anyone tell you differently!

I think good will flow in the wake of Tuesday's tragedy. It already has. And I believe, as well, that there is some meaning to be found in the midst of the suffering that has come upon us. Further, I know somewhere, somehow, there is something redemptive about it, for God's purpose to redeem works through all things, always. But, my friends, don't for a moment confuse that position with one that assigns responsibility or intent to God. Jerry Falwell couldn't be more wrong! Did Yahweh bring the Hebrews out to destroy them? Of course not! No less has the Spirit toyed sadistically with us!

My first point today is: God is like that mother who bends down to where her child grieves, drawing the disappointment and despair of life gone terribly wrong unto her breast. In her we have hope. My second point is: Those who assign responsibility for Tuesday's carnage to God's angry revenge don't know Moses and haven't met Jesus. And if they're going to call themselves Christian, then they'd dang well better learn the way of compassion! And my third point today is: It is tough these days to follow Jesus.

I referred earlier to the God of the Exodus with whom Moses counseled as an anthropomorphic God, reflecting human character and emotion. And how very human it is to want to strike out when hurt, as we have been. It is to be expected then that we are hearing language now of revenge, retribution, and retaliation coming from within and without. (I'm as ready to go after bin Laden as anyone!) But as Christians, when we know God as "The Tender Care That Nothing Be Lost," then we must take the "Nothing" seriously and say no more words of hate; remembering as Gandhi, King, and Christ have taught that to refrain from revenge is a spiritual discipline and rule of faith (albeit a tough one) to which this day we are being called. Listen to Dr. King's words:

> Darkness cannot drive out darkness; only light can do that. Hate cannot drive out hate; only love can do that. Hate multiplies hate, violence multiplies violence, and toughness multiplies toughness in a descending spiral of destruction. The chain reaction of evil—hate begetting hate, wars producing more wars—must be broken, or we shall be plunged unto the dark abyss of annihilation. (Rev. Dr. Martin Luther King, Jr., *Strength To Love,* 1963.)

The truth is, we don't know where our political and military leaders will take us. But as religious people, as believers, we do know every precious life matters. It matters very much indeed. And we know, too, the God of all life will be grieved more if others are lost. May the Spirit strengthen us then in the resolve of peace. Amen.

Single-minded

William J. O'Malley, S.J.

William O'Malley teaches theology and English at Fordham Preparatory School in The Bronx, New York. He is the author of numerous books on Catholicism. This sermon was preached on the campus of Fordham University shortly after the tragedy that occurred on September 11.

A young woman knocked on my dorm room door Tuesday night and asked the question we've probably all asked ourselves: "Why are people so evil?" I didn't have a ready answer. Who could? So the rest of the evening and Wednesday morning I pondered that.

As Atticus Finch suggests in *To Kill a Mockingbird,* I tried to put myself into the skin of one of those pilots and see the world and life from inside him. He was probably a quite intelligent man, able to handle the enormous complexity of flying a transcontinental jet plane. Doubtlessly, as a Muslim, he prayed five times a day, which is more often than most of us do, to the same God. He was utterly devoted to a cause, which was crystal clear to him—without any doubts or shadows or hesitations. He was, in a word, single-minded.

He was as single-minded as the crusaders who hacked their way to Jerusalem in the name of Jesus. As single-minded as the inquisitors who perpetrated unutterable suffering in the name of the God who suffered for us all. As single-minded as the revolutionaries who rampaged through France decapitating any priest or nun or anyone with a claim to noble blood. As single-minded as the Nazis who obediently herded human beings, as if they had no more value than cattle, and gassed and incinerated them as even less valuable than cattle. As single-minded as Kamikaze pilots who dove their planes into American battleships. As single-minded as Senator Joseph McCarthy, who ruined countless human lives in order to root out members of the Communist Party. As single-minded as the Ku Klux Klan and Black Panthers. As single-minded as rebels who blow up busses of schoolchildren as a legitimate means to achieve what they totally believe is a righteous cause. As single-minded as the El Salvador government that sponsored a poster campaign: "Be a patriot. Kill a priest." As single-minded as the gangsta rappers who scream the answer is in killing police.

In every single one of those horrific situations, including what happened in America on Tuesday, every single person involved believed what he or she was engaged in was a righteous, justified, holy action. No doubts, no qualifications, no legitimate contrary arguments. All the problems of our lives are rooted in a single cause: It's all the fault of the infidels, the Jews, the communists, the rich, the cops, the blacks, the whites, the Americans. They were utterly, unshakably—even in the face of death—certain.

My classroom is papered with slogans. One of them says, "The great sin is certitude, the great virtue is doubt." Another says: "The less you know, the more certain you can be." The people who commit human atrocities are not evil in themselves, the way cyanide is evil and cholera is evil. They are single-minded. Their inflexible convictions are incapable of seeing the complexities of human life. By their very single-mindedness, they are simple-minded. As George says to Lenny in *Of Mice and Men,* "It ain't wicked people that causes all the problems. It's dumb people." Adolf Eichmann, who facilitated the transport of all the Jews in Europe to extermination camps, and Lt. William Calley, who led a platoon of soldiers to slaughter 360 helpless old men and women and infants at My Lai in Vietnam, weren't evil. They were single-minded; that is, simple, gullible, stupid. It's the age-old distinction between the sinner and the sin.

Already there are stories of people trashing American Arab mosques and businesses, just as they did German Jewish synagogues and businesss in the 1930s. Plain, simple, stupid people.

They had never been led to get into other people's skin and look around at life from their viewpoint. They were led to believe that the God who created life exults in death. They had never learned empathy—for the pain, the hopes, the bewilderment— of other human beings. Kill all compassion, all fellow-feeling with the infidel, the heretic, the kike, the kraut, the nigger, the honkey, the spick, the slope, the faggot, and chaos is inescapable. The beast in us is unleashed.

The reason for the existence of this school is not to get you into good colleges, to prepare you to be an attractive job candidate, to pave the yellow brick road to the American Dream. You're here to learn how to think, how to reason, how to see and feel the complex evidence—even if it conflicts with your heartfelt beliefs—to learn how to put the evidence into a logical sequence so you can draw a balanced, personal conclusion and ask someone wiser to critique it. We're here to invite you to ever more complex mind-challenges, to read novels and plays so you can get into other peoples' skins and walk around in them a while, live a thousand lives before you set out to live your own life. The most basic purpose of this institution is to train men and women who are not single-minded, not simple-minded fanatics, but people governed by the objective truth, by our common humanity, and—one hopes—by the selflessness of the cross.

Tuesday completely fissioned our American complacency. The same single-mindedness governs our Monopoly capitalism and global popular culture: Profit justifies everything. The same single-mindedness roams our own streets: Violence will solve it all. Nothing will solve it all, not even universal literacy. We have to go beyond literacy, which is only a tool to understanding humanity, to seeing the complex truth in the midst of an even more complex background of self-interests and different agendas. We invite you to become fully human beings and, we hope, open-minded, open-hearted, open-handed Christians.

Toward the end of *A Man for All Seasons,* Thomas More's jailer tries to excuse himself for having taken away More's family. He's just a nobody, following orders; he says, "You got to understand, sir. I'm just a plain simple man." And More sinks to his knees moaning, "Sweet Jesus! These plain, simple men!"

The Shaking of the Foundations

Timothy L. Carson

Timothy Carson is senior pastor of Webster Groves Christian Church in St. Louis, Missouri. This sermon was preached there on Sunday, September 16, 2001.

Luke 14:1–10

It has been said that each soul is like a battlefield and the most important wars are always fought there, first of all and last of all. If that is true, our hearts have inwardly mirrored the outward tragedy, which we have come to know all too well.

Not a one of us has escaped the roller coaster of powerful emotions that has brought forth the best in us and the worst in us. So it is when people are thrust into an unthinkable, dastardly, shattering calamity. And that such a tragedy would be intentional, well, that rubs salt into the gaping wound.

Which one of us has not reeled from day to day, hour to hour, when we witnessed what seemed to be something off a motion picture set? So much terrible human suffering. So much terror and fear and confusion and grief and helplessness. And then when we discovered the infamy of it all, the pure evil, there was hardly anything left but blind rage and hurt.

How in the world could a person, group, or movement hate us intensely enough to commit mass murder of innocent civilians? On the political or cultural or religious level it is complex, but not impossible to explain. And certainly in the future we will need to dedicate much more energy to the exploration of those issues.

An act of terror is always motivated by anger, fear, and desperation. And, in this case, a religious ideology. Its purpose is to create the same kind of terrible feelings in the victims. In these days immediately following the atrocity, we all experienced exactly that. But not only that. On the surface, our violators succeeded: They took life, they destroyed national symbols, they proved that we were more vulnerable than we thought, they disrupted commerce and travel and communications and family life. Yes, on those levels they succeeded. They took advantage of our free society and executed a remarkable plan. But how little they really know about us.

What we also have witnessed and even felt rising within our own spirits is heroism, courage, compassion, resolve, solidarity, faith, and even hope. To be sure, we mourn and grieve; but unlike the Twin Towers, we shall not collapse. From under the debris of calamity a tender green shoot is already pushing its way up to the surface. And it will not be hindered.

Will we address security issues in a world now unsafe in different ways? Of course.

Will we seek justice in the face of tyranny? We believe we will.

Will we strive to contribute to the increase of peace and harmony in the world, eliminating oppression—even our own—wherever it is humanly possible? It is our fervent hope.

Will we respond in ways that will not cause yet more evil and more suffering of the innocent? That is yet to be seen.

What is unexpected here, what was totally unanticipated by the murderers, is the moral fiber of our nation. And that fiber, when it is at its best, is wrapped and bound by the religious bonds of hope and trust in God.

Now we are faced with the daunting reality of our own freedom. We are totally free to respond to this tragedy in a multitude of ways. And the shaking foundations within us keep us oscillating from one to another.

On the one hand, we could descend into our lower natures and come to resemble the very enemy we deplore. We could sink in the quicksand of hatred and stay there. It is possible that we could permanently mistrust every Middle Eastern–looking person and even treat innocent persons hatefully because they fit a certain profile. Our fear could do that.

In the words of the Prayer of St. Francis, could we become an instrument of God's peace? That is a hard question to answer, especially now. We can hold in prayer every passenger on every doomed plane, every worker in the crumbling, blazing buildings, every firefighter or rescue worker or survivor or average American glued to the TV; but how can we become an instrument of God's peace now? You see, it is easy to become an agent of God's peace when all around us is harmonious. The test of our spiritual mettle comes in the time of trial.

I've heard it said that being a Christian makes such times so much more bearable, even survivable. And, in one sense, I think that is quite true. The power of God at work within us leads us in inscrutable ways—ways beyond our imagining. But I also have to say that being a practicing Christian also makes things much harder. It is harder because of the moral dimensions of our faith—a faith that makes particular claims about God and sin and relation to neighbor, a faith that includes the particular teachings of Jesus, and those teachings do not necessarily make it easier to endure such a calamity. Let me give you an example.

On Wednesday we had a prayer service, and at the close of the service we shared the Lord's Prayer together. We all did quite well, petition by petition—"Thy kingdom come, thy will be done…Give us this day our daily bread." We even prayed loud and clear, "Forgive us our sins…" But when the petition came, "…as we forgive those who sin against us," there was an almost immediate silence in the room. We choked on our own prayer because we couldn't pray it.

What this reminds us of is that there is merit to praying universal prayers of the ages—not just what we are inclined to feel at the moment—because they lead us to pray what we need and must pray even when our hearts are not in it. I'll keep trying to pray it until I *can* pray it.

But even more, it reminds us how being a Christian does not necessarily make things easier for us. In fact, being a Christian is frequently at cross-purposes with a huge quantity of what we are happening to feel at any given moment. One of the most important things about a religious tradition is that it reveals truth that is bigger than you are. We often have to grow into shoes that are too big for us.

I have to confess that the greatest struggle of these past few days for me—after dealing with the pure shock and grief—was how to reconcile my Christian faith with my feelings about the *animals* who did this. There were times when I knew how far away I was from God and just had to say to myself, *Wait until you can be faithful again.* I even felt this distance in different places in my body, in my brain. Some animalistic survival instinct that wanted to lash out was in competition with Jesus on the cross saying, "Father forgive them, they do not know what they do."

No, if your religious faith is worth its salt, it not only brings you incredible consolation in times of trouble, but also puts you in terrible moral conflict.

On the one hand, my instinctual response was to think that nobody had seen suffering like this before. But then my faith awakened an awareness of people throughout the rest of the world who endure this scope of malicious violence all the time; and it is not episodal—it is constant and chronic. There are genocides out there. Now I will know some of what it is like, now that my glass cocoon of privilege has been shattered.

In a way, faith is making it easier and harder at the same time.

This week members of Interfaith Partnership gathered to plan an interfaith service of prayer. I have to tell you that both the hardest and most hopeful thing was being together. There we were—Catholic, Protestant, Jewish, and Muslim—and there was that unspoken tension and suffering as the Muslim Imam joined in our deliberation. How painful it is for those of us who suspect radical Muslims of terror to trust. How painful it is for peaceful Muslims who are ashamed of the violence of their fanatical brothers and frightened by the hatefulness of some in our community toward them to meet with us.

You see, it might not be *better* but it certainly would be *easier* if we didn't feel any moral obligation from our faith to be peacemakers. We could just wash our hands of it and go down the road. But we don't have that option—not if we are practicing Christians.

And what about forgiveness? That is perhaps the hardest issue for us to address. There is little difference among individuals or groups or communities as they have to face the ones who have violated them. Regardless of the scope—whether it is those who lost family in Oklahoma City, or in Poland in one of the death camps in World War II, or in a drive-by shooting in St. Louis—the questions remain: How is forgiveness possible, and who shall determine that it is?

For the Jew, forgiveness is tied to moral justice—and when proper confession of wrong and reparations are made, forgiveness is a possibility. For the Muslim, forgiveness is primarily an act of mercy by which one extends something the other doesn't deserve. For the Christian, forgiveness is rooted in the forgiveness offered by God to us, graphically known in our own violation and sin as we gaze upon Christ's cross. Indeed, the Lord's Prayer sets it up: "Forgive us our sins as we forgive the sins of those who sin against us." Is that possible?

What is not possible is for one person to tell another person when this should take place. Only the violated one decides when forgiveness is possible and offered. It is a moment of grace in which the spirit of non-forgiveness is taken away.

Even though we have the Christian teaching about forgiveness, you and I can never say to another, "Okay, now is the time for you to forgive." That takes place on God's timetable as a grace.

You see how much harder being a Christian makes things?

One's greatest hope could be that in the future, in a time beyond where we are right now, all parties will realize the destructiveness, fruitlessness, and evil of all violence, oppression, greed, and hate. If justice means making relationships right and equitable again, and if forgiveness is the wiping clean of the slate in order that people can begin again by the grace of God, the best hope we could realize would be the appearance of both— justice and forgiveness. If we can hold both of those liberating powers in our hands simultaneously, you never know where we might end up.

I don't know, but God does...and we have to trust that.

When you think about it, the people who boarded those jets, or went to work in one of those buildings, or reported for rescue duty, and who died, had no idea that Tuesday was to be the last day of their lives. But then again, we don't know when the final bell will toll for us either. As surely as you and I are here today, we had better face that inevitability. We are not immortal, and when folks come to that realization in their lives it often sends them stumbling toward God. I pray that is the case for each person here today. Stumbling toward God. Lost ones stumbling into the arms of the Shepherd.

How in God's Name?

Jon M. Walton

Jon M. Walton is senior pastor of First Presbyterian Church in New York City, where this sermon was preached on Sunday, September 16, 2001.

Isaiah 40; Matthew 5:1–12; Romans 8:18–19, 31–39

What word is there to say that has not already been said? What cry to heaven has not already been raised that has said so much more than any cry we might raise? For days this avenue outside our doors was silent, and the silence said it all.

There were screams of sirens, of course, echoes of the screams that came when the Towers fell, the terror of our disbelief that continues to reverberate on the walls of these stone canyons and probably always will. We now know what the prophet Ezekiel meant when he said, "I sat there among them, stunned, for seven days" (Ezekiel 3:15b).

This week the doors of the church have been open, and we have embraced a city, a nation, and, in fact, a world of mourners of every imaginable faith. Many with soulful doubts have sat in these pews stunned and offered up prayers, and looked for help, and longed for an explanation, because we are all waiting for answers to the unanswerable questions that are in our hearts.

Why did this happen? What is the meaning of it? Where was God? And how will we go on with life now that we have seen and experienced what we have?

And, of course, we are also left with the impossible question of what kind of evil in this world stalks with such stealth and violence that it would rob all of us of our simpler lives and rip from our arms our mothers and sisters and daughters, our fathers and brothers and sons, our husbands, wives, partners, and lovers, fianc…s, and co-workers, the neighbors in our own buildings.

They got up with us like every other day on Tuesday. They walked the dog, or jogged in the park, got dressed, and took the Number "1" or the "E" or the PATH train dawn to the World Trade Center, and then took the elevator up to the 100th or the 78th or the 45th floor to begin a day of work. The usual stack of papers was waiting for them, the list of calls to return, the computer screens flashing the usual figures from the Tokyo exchange, and the London trading. It was the same old thing Tuesday morning. Another day, another dollar. The same kind of day as yesterday, it seemed, and all the days before.

But all our yesterdays and all our tomorrows will never be the same because of what happened that day. We have seen enough of the sickening sight, the plane banking at full speed into Tower Number 2. The sight at the end of this street looking south that none of us will ever forget. It is enough to remember without seeing it again in replay after ghastly replay.

All week long the city has poured into these doors. Our staff, my colleagues, so many volunteers, our custodians, our deacons, and members of goodwill have come to help us all get through it. More have offered help than we know how to deploy. E-mails from all around the world have come in, with offers to drop everything and come to New York to help. But the help we have needed most is the help we have received from the firefighters and police and medical community, who have given every measure of selflessness this week, including, the last full measure of their devotion.

Mountains of clothing have been donated and rivers of blood have been stored up, as we have kept watch together and comforted one another as best we could.

Five of our extended church family are unaccounted for: our church secretary Charlotte Wallace's husband, Peter, who worked on the 100th floor of the North Tower; our church receptionist Keith Blacknall's nephew, David Williams, who was an engineer on the 45th floor of the South Tower; Ginger Ormiston who was on the 78th floor of Tower Number 2, who was last seen evacuating with a co-worker as she called her husband Jim to let him know she was on her way out; David Rivers, a parent who has been active in our nursery school and who headed the auction last year; and Janet Gustafson, mother of two children, whom most of our own kids in this church have known as a teacher of three- and four-year-olds.

I name them by name before you because it is important to remember that that is how they, and we, are known by God, unique and special, beloved and desired, treasured and adored. The grief that tears at our hearts for their absence from us is multiplied five thousand times over—a burden of sorrow that this city has borne in what has become its finest hour of courage and self-sacrifice in the face of infamy.

To say the obvious, peace does not come on Earth when unsuspecting thousands are murdered at the hands of zealots who have been promised direct access to heaven for dying in a holy war that is utterly unholy. Justice cannot be achieved on Earth for Palestinians, or Israelis, or for any nation or cause when injustice, evil, and revenge are the means of achieving its end.

Murder is murder by whatever name, and the cycle of violence on which hatred feeds is an insatiable lion. There is no end to the burning of such fury. If all these years of injustice and endless bloodshed in the Middle East have not taught us that, what have they taught us?

This is not the Sunday to lay upon our grieving shoulders the burden of the obvious truth that we as a nation have all too often turned a deaf ear to the cries of Palestinian people who have sought justice for wrongful injustices. That is not the point on this day of mourning and sadness, with the smell of smoke still in our clothing and the clouds of embers still stinging our eyes.

It is also not a day for the kind of reckless comments made by the well-heeled prophets of Christian fundamentalism who have laid this tragedy at the doors of moral decadence.

Television evangelists Jerry Falwell and Pat Robertson announced on Thursday that "God gave us what we deserve." "The abortionists," Falwell said, "have got to bear some blame for this because God will not be mocked…The feminists, and the gays, and the lesbians…the ACLU, People for the American Way," Falwell said, "helped make this happen."[1]

It is such an outrageous claim to make that I fear dignifying it by responding to it, but such Christian fascism must not go unanswered. The literalism and fundamentalism out of which Robertson and Falwell speak is neither Christian nor Christlike, and in its perversion of Christianity, it is cut from the same cloth as the perversion of Islam that is used by bin Laden and his ilk to murder others. Terrorists who trade on violence have nothing to do with the true heart of Islam at all, but with the love of bloodshed and the mustering of power.

While a few Christian fundamentalists like Falwell and Robertson seem ready to say more than they know, what most of us have been struck by is the inexplicability of what we have witnessed, the silence of it all—not just the silence of the streets this week, but the eerie emptiness of the avenues, the hushed speechlessness of people who do not know what to say.

What has been especially unnerving has been the apparent silence of God. The lack of word from on high. The quietness of the heavens that took all week until Thursday night to rage in its thunder and begin to cry; so in shock was heaven itself, apparently like us, at the impossibility of such a thing becoming possible. Somehow, I think the clouds themselves were searching all week for those Towers, roaming the sky in sympathy, looking for something prouder and taller than what is left to nuzzle.

In spite of all the talking that is being done on television hour after hour, the constant recapping and reviewing and replaying, there is, at the heart of this tragedy, a kind of silence that defies an answer.

It's the silence inside us that we feel when we see the faces that are being pasted on subway walls and kiosks on the street, the pictures held in the hands of tearful relatives who stand at the Chelsea piers and line the barricades at St. Vincent's and wait in silence at Union Square. Who of us would rob these heartsick ones of the hope these pictures hold, and yet who of us believes that they are coming back? There is a silence inside us that we can hardly bear.

I worry for the cries for blood that have broken the silence prematurely. The majority opinion calls for the swift and heavy hand of the most powerful nation on Earth to be unleashed on some small Middle Eastern principality. One Israeli partisan being interviewed the other evening recommended an American invasion of not only Afghanistan, but also Iran, Iraq, Syria, Libya and anybody else that gets in the way!

There is no question that there must be a response. Justice cries for it. But we must pray that those who are charged with such decisions, our president and national leaders, do not in their actions lead us as a nation to become the same as our enemies. We are a society of justice and a nation intent on peace. We must not at this grave hour abandon that which is best in our ideals and most dear to our identity as a free nation.

The cries of those who died so unjustly demand that justice be done. But the threat that we will invade other nations and set loose upon them wanton destruction out of the rage that we feel in our sorrow will not bring back those who have died so unfairly, and will only fuel the flames of violence that may make us less secure, not more so. Don't we all hope that what justice is done may be more measured and strategic than that?

My dear friend Anne Ledbetter, mother of three children and a colleague in ministry who continues to serve the church in Delaware that I left only a month ago, wrote to me Friday something I cannot get out of my mind. "In some ways," she said, "I am more frightened by radical, militant patriotism and harsh threats of retribution than I am of future air travel and the shattered view that we live in a safe [society]."

Like everybody else, deep in my heart, somewhere, mixed with all the grieving there is anger and a rage so deep that it scares even me that I feel it. I know that there is a part of me that wants to get back at the villains, a dark side that would like to send in the troops, and open up the bomb bays, and reset the missiles for very specific targets. I imagine that with satellites so strong that they can read license plates from miles into the stratosphere it should be no problem to pinpoint the exact location of the dens of iniquity, the very lairs and hiding places of those who are responsible. I have that in me, I know it, and it is abroad in the land this day, this very worst of bloodthirstiness that is at the heart of our broken nature as sinful people.

And then I catch myself and realize that if we, as a people, become like those who have harmed us—ruthless, lawless, evil and cunning in our stealth, without care for the lives of innocent human beings whom we dismiss as the inevitable waste of "collateral damage"—we will ourselves have allowed evil to take over the world, and all the goodness and worthiness that we have as a nation will have been lost in the ghastly plumes of smoke that have risen over us this week.

There were reports at week's end of cruelty and meanness to people of Middle Eastern descent in this nation. There is graffiti written on telephone kiosks and scrawled on the walls of public places here in the Village threatening harm to Arabs and death to Muslims. My heart sinks at the pity of it! If nothing else, the sight of those towers burning is a symbol to us all of the futility of doing violence to one another in whatever form.

At last it comes down to this, the question that will not stop haunting me day in and day out, that wakes me in the morning and troubles me into the night, the question of how in the name of God such a thing could have been done. How could anyone do this in the name of Allah, or Adonai, or Yahweh, or God

Almighty, the Great Mysterious One who is the Creator of
Heaven and of Earth? By whatever name you call God, how
could anyone imagine that God could be pleased by such a
horror? What kind of God is that?

Most assuredly not the God I know. The God I know is a
God whose heart was broken Tuesday morning, whose heart
has been broken so many times before, who weeps for us, and
longs for us to end our warring ways. The God I know is a God
of compassion and love; the God who gave us everything, the
Earth and the heavens, the sky and the sun, the moon and the
stars, and who delighted in it all, and called it good; a God who
has given us each other as a blessing to be treasured, who knows
us through and through and loves us still and all.

How then, you ask, in God's name, could such a thing as
this have happened? Could not God have stopped it? Could
not God have prevented those zealots from doing the things
they did? The only thing I can come up with is that God has
been trying. God did not mean for us to have things come out
this way. One thing is for sure, and that is that nothing that I
saw on the horizon as I stood out on the sidewalk with everyone
else last Tuesday morning looking down Fifth Avenue to those
blazing towers at the end of our line of sight—nothing that I
saw there looked anything like the will of God to me.

To imagine that God intends human suffering, that God
wills a terrorist to commandeer a plane and take the lives of
thousands of people who were going about a day's work as if it
were any other day, is to misunderstand God altogether—God,
whose eye is on the sparrow, who has numbered every hair on
our heads. That was not God's will that I saw there blazing in
the sky. That was something quite the opposite.

It was William Sloane Coffin who said on the occasion of
his son's death some years ago that, "God's heart was the first of
all our hearts to break."[2] And so I think it was again on Tuesday
morning. God's heart was the first of all our hearts to break—
the first to feel the impact of the glass shattering, the first to
know the burning of the fire, the first to feel the collapsing of

the steel, the first to receive into those everlasting arms the bodies of the wounded and the dying.

I cannot presume to speak for God. No one with such imperfect sight or understanding as we possess on Earth can do so—except to witness to the fact that God has given us One who has taught us a still more excellent way than we have ever yet been able to live. One who has held up to us a better possibility for our living than we have ever yet achieved. He who took upon himself the pain and suffering and sin of the world, and bore the worst the world could do for the sake of the best that God intended—Jesus Christ, in whose name we have gathered today and by whose love we are drawn together.

In him, we know that the evil of this world will not have the last say; that goodness and mercy and peace shall reign some day, even if not today; that one day, swords will be beaten into plowshares and spears into pruning hooks and nation shall not lift up sword against nation anymore. Then shall come to pass that city seen by John, a city yet to come, with gleaming towers and peaceful people, a city of justice and salaam, a city of kindness and shalom, a city coming down out of heaven from God, prepared as a bride adorned for her husband. In that city, God will be with us. God will wipe every tear from our eyes. And death will be no more.

Keep in your hearts the vision of a city like that and it will come! It will come!

Notes

[1] *Washington Post,* September 14, 2001, John F. Harris, staff writer.
[2] From "Alex's Death," a sermon preached at the Riverside Church in the city of New York.

Looking through the Glass

David A. Shirey

David Shirey is currently serving as interim senior minister of Southport Christian Church in Indianapolis, Indiana. This sermon was preached there on Sunday, September 16, 2001.

Where were you when you heard? Tuesday's horrors have etched onto the calendar of our memories another date that goes down in infamy. We remember where we were when we receive the chilling news of our lives. For you who are old enough, do you remember where you were on December 7, 1941? Pearl Harbor. A quarter-century century later, do you remember where you were on November 22, 1963, when President John F. Kennedy was shot? When Challenger exploded into the Florida sky, I was at a meeting at Vanderbilt Divinity School in Nashville. I can see exactly where I was sitting. Where were you when you first heard of the Murrah Federal Building in Oklahoma City and what had happened to it? There are dates and the images accompanying them that are engraved on our minds forever.

We are not alone. Our forebears in the faith, God's people Israel, had dark dates seared into their souls as well. Evil—even evil on a grand and hideous scale—has been around for a long, long time. Its effects are not forgotten. Take Jeremiah the prophet; for him, the darkest date of all was 587 B.C. As long as he lived, he could not erase from his memory images of Jerusalem's destruction. The Babylonians had laid siege to the city for long months. Finally, the city's walls were surmounted. Its buildings were brought to ruin and set afire. The people were taken captive into exile and, as a final dagger to the very heart of the people, the Temple was destroyed. Jerusalem was no more. There were no video cameras that captured the onslaught. No photographs of the Temple in ruins. But we do have Jeremiah's memoirs of those dark days preserved for us in the pages of scripture. They are aptly titled "Lamentations." As the title suggests, its pages are tear-streaked, anguish-filled, wrenching. Reading through Jeremiah's Lamentations as I did in this sanctuary on Tuesday morning, you recognize that the man never forgot where he was the day the city was brought to ruin.

We heard a selection of Jeremiah's lament read to us by Bill, Steven, Dick, Joan, and Gene:

- What words did Jeremiah use to describe the trouble he'd seen?

  "How lonely sits the city
  that once was full of people!
  How like a widow she has become,
  she that was great among the nations!"
  (Lamentations 1:1)

- And how did such a sight make him feel?

  "See, O LORD, how distressed I am;
  my stomach churns,
  my heart is wrung within me,...
  My eyes are spent with weeping...
  because of the destruction of my people."
  (Lamentations 1:20; 2:11)

- What else did he see?

> *"All who pass along the way*
> clap their hands at you;
> they hiss and wag their heads
> at daughter Jerusalem;...
> they cry: "We have devoured her!
> Ah, this is the day we longed for;
> *at last we have seen it!"*
> (Lamentations 2:15–16)

- And what did you do, Jeremiah?

> *"I called on your name, O LORD,*
> from the depths of the pit;...
> 'Give me relief!'...
> You have seen the wrong done to me, O LORD;
> judge my cause.
> You have seen all their malice,
> *all their plots against me."*
> (Lamentations 3:55–56, 59–60)

Reading those words on Tuesday and hearing them again this morning, I wondered if Jeremiah's Lamentations were written from Jerusalem in 587 B.C. or from New York City (or Washington, D.C.) in 2001.

I want you to know, however, that though Jeremiah's Lamentations over Jerusalem were the *first* words that spoke to me on Tuesday morning, they were not the *last* words! I want you to know that though I entered this sanctuary Tuesday morning a lost man, I left it with a renewed sense of direction. And to think that the transformation came about because I needed some light. Literally (but also, God knows, *figuratively* speaking), I needed some light. It was dim in the sanctuary and, not knowing how to turn the lights on, I went to look for Larry, our custodian, to assist me. I found him and he said he'd be right with me. I returned to the sanctuary to wait for him. As I came to the doors, instead of going in, I stood and looked *through* the glass until suddenly my eyes fixed *on* the glass itself, namely, on the words that are etched into the glass. I have admired the beauty of the etched glass doors leading into this sanctuary in my brief time with you, but it was not until Tuesday morning that I actually looked at them closely. What I saw brought the light of God's Word into the darkness of our world, which is why I say that though Jeremiah's Lamentations were the first words that spoke to me on Tuesday, they were not the last words. The last words that spoke to me were the words I saw etched upon the glass. This morning, thanks be to God, they are etched as well upon my mind and heart and soul.

May I tell you some of the words I saw as I looked through glass? I saw the words "Fear no evil." I know where those words come from. I know what words come before them ("Though I walk through the valley of the shadow of the death"), and I know what words come after them ("For thou art with me. Thy rod and thy staff they comfort me"). Thanks be to God for my fifth grade Sunday school teacher, Mrs. Tims, who had us memorize the Twenty-third Psalm as children. I tell you, those words are etched not just in the glass but on my mind and in my heart and on my soul!

Looking through the glass I saw the words "Yes, Jesus loves me" and the words "They are weak but he is strong." I know those words, and I know that my children know those words. Indeed, those words and the melody that go with them are etched on glass, mind, heart, and soul.

Looking through the glass I saw the words "Precious Lord, take my hand." I know those words and that hymn! I promise you those words are there [pointing to glass], and here [pointing to head], and here [pointing to heart].

Looking through the glass, across the very top, my eyes saw the words, "…void and darkness covered the face of…" I know that one, too. It's from the Creation story. "In the beginning when God created the heavens and the earth, the earth was a formless *void and darkness covered the face of* the deep" (Genesis 1:1–3). I know that story. It's etched in my mind. What's more, I know the Spirit of God was hovering over the face of the deep.

Then God said, "Let there be light," and there was light. With that, God proceeded to bring forth order out of that primordial chaos.

As I looked through the glass and saw those words, I realized anew that ours is a faith that allows us to look at places which can only be described as "formless voids" and yet believe with a fierce faith that the same Spirit that hovered over the chaos on that first day is present this day. Bringing order out of chaos; shining light into the darkness; ours is a God of beginnings *and new beginnings!*

Jeremiah knew that, too. You see, even in Lamentations lament is not the last word! Looking not through the glass but through the eyes of faith, Jeremiah lifted his eyes to the One who is able even to resurrect ruins.

- How did you put it, Jeremiah?

  "This I call to mind,
  and therefore I have hope:
  The steadfast love of the Lord
  never ceases,
  his mercies never come to an end."
  (Lamentations 3:21–22)

- And then the voice which had earlier lamented breaks forth into song:

  "Morning by morning new mercies I see,
  Great is thy faithfulness."
  (Lamentations 3:23; "Great Is Thy Faithfulness")

This is to testify that in looking through the glass—and looking through God's Word—I have found "strength for today and bright hope for tomorrow." We have reason for lamentation, yes, but as people of faith we have reason, too, for bold hope.

Listen. I returned to this sanctuary on Friday noon, and as I sat, I lifted my eyes. This time I saw the cross, and it dawned on me that the last time I had been in a sanctuary on a Friday noon was five months ago. It was a Friday in April. In fact, it was a

Friday at the end of a week when deceit, stealth, lies, violence, suffering, and terror had conspired to take an innocent life. In a word, all hell had broken loose during the week leading up to the last time I had been in a sanctuary on a Friday noon. It was on Good Friday!

But the memory of that was all I needed to look forward to coming back to this place today. Because you see, the story that is etched upon my mind and in my heart is that though there are days such as Tuesday and weeks such as the one that culminated on Friday noon, we have a God whose workweek ends not on Tuesday or Friday, but on Sunday! The story as I've come to know and believe with all my heart says that the Sunday following Good Friday is the Day of Resurrection! It may not seem like Easter, but if you look through the glass, through God's Word, it is well and right for us to claim this day and the days to follow for good purposes…for God's purposes.

Just before we came into the sanctuary, Gene pulled me aside and said, "David, I want you to come and look at something in the courtyard." So I went with her. When we got to the window, she pointed and said, "Would you look at that!"

"Look at what, Gene?"

"Right there. I planted that Easter lily last spring. It's blooming this morning!"

Indeed, it was. So I will say it again: It may not seem like Easter, but if you look through the glass, through God's Word, it is well and right for us to claim this day and the days to follow for good purposes…for God's purposes.

So shall we?

Earlier this week I heard a reporter say, "We're waiting for someone to step up and claim responsibility for what has happened. Who will claim responsibility for such murder and mayhem?"

I'd like to turn that question around this morning and ask, "Who will step up and claim responsibility for the redeeming of this sin-scarred world? Who will claim responsibility for bringing forth new life?" I ask that question because there is etched in my mind this morning images and words of those who have already accepted such responsibility these past days. I give thanks to God for them and their witness!

Who will accept responsibility for rescuing the perishing?

Thanks be to God for the brave firefighters, police officers, and rescue workers who have answered the call, many at the cost of their lives. Their act has etched these words on my mind: "No one has greater love than this, to lay down one's life for one's friends" (John 15:13).

Who will accept responsibility for bearing witness to God's desire for reconciliation among the people of this sorely divided world?

Thanks be to God for the National Day of Prayer Service at the National Cathedral where Catholic, Protestant, Jewish, and Muslim clerics joined hand and heart in one accord, calling upon the God of Abraham, the God of Muhammad, the God and Father of our Lord Jesus Christ for peace. Their witness brought to my mind words that are etched in my heart: "My house shall be called a house of prayer for all peoples" (Isaiah 56:7). "In days to come all the nations shall stream to [the Lord's house]…They shall beat their swords into plowshares, and their spears into pruning hooks; nation shall not lift up sword against nation, neither shall they learn war any more" (Isaiah 2:2–4).

Who will be a voice of restraint and reason when righteous anger and rightful demands for justice threaten to boil over into hateful rhetoric and hateful actions against any and all Arab and Muslim peoples, including fellow Americans and innocent civilians in other nations?

I give thanks for local, state, and national leaders, including President Bush, who have sternly denounced such scapegoating of people and who I pray are carefully weighing the scope and target of our nation's response so that we do not become the evil we deplore. "Blessed are the peacemakers, for they will be called children of God" (Matthew 5:9).

"Who will step up and claim responsibility for the redeeming of this sin-scarred world? Who will claim responsibility for bringing forth new life?"

None of us will forget where we were on September 11, 2001, when we heard the news. But I for one will remember where I was when I was given new hope and heard the call to a renewed commitment to being a healer, a reconciler, a striver for peace with justice. I remember exactly where I was when I gave myself again to God's redeeming work:

I was looking through the glass at the words.

I was in the sanctuary of Southport Christian Church.

It was on a Tuesday morning.

It was on a Friday noon.

It was on a Sunday morning.

It was a new day in the life of the world and God's Spirit was hovering over the face of the deep.

O God, let there be light!

Elusive Honor

Pablo A. Jiménez

Pablo A. Jiménez is the National Pastor for Hispanic Ministries of the Christian Church (Disciples of Christ) in the United States and Canada. This sermon was preached at a special memorial service held at La Hermosa Christian Church in New York City during the Northeast Hispanic Convention on Sunday, October 14, 2001.

Genesis 4:1–10

Recently, I discovered a small Middle Eastern restaurant close to my office in Indianapolis. With glee, I saw that they served "baklava," a dessert made with assorted nuts, brown sugar, and phyllo dough. While I struggled with the temptation to indulge, the restaurant's owner looked at me with curiosity and asked me: "Where do you come from?" I answered: "I come from Puerto Rico, an island in the Caribbean." Surprised, he told me: "You look Middle Eastern. You must have some Middle Eastern blood in you, given that the Moors lived in Spain for so long. I am from Lebanon. In any case, we all come from the Mediterranean basin."

Yes, every Hispanic person has some Mediterranean heritage. This explains the points of contact between Hispanic culture and biblical cultures. For example, the Latino people have a high sense of honor, as the Hebrew and Arab peoples do.

Honor is a key value in the Bible. It can be very positive, but it can also have negative consequences. It is positive when it inspires us to act justly, to keep our word, and to allow our highest ideals to guide our everyday conduct. However, it can become a negative value when it inspires false pride and vengeance. As a matter of fact, a false sense of honor inspired the first tragedy in the Bible: The murder of Abel at the hands of his brother Cain.

According to the sacred scriptures Adam and Eve, the first couple of human beings, had two sons (Genesis 4:1). The older one was Cain, who eventually became a farmer. The younger one was Abel, who became a shepherd (v. 2). In time, Cain and Abel came of age. With maturity came obligation, particularly the responsibility to participate in worship. As we know, in ancient Israel human sacrifices and the presentation of the first fruits of labor were part of worship. These were "offerings" that believers laid on God's altar.

According to the Genesis account, Cain presented to God some of the fruits of his fields (v. 3). By the same token, Abel presented a firstborn of his flock (v. 4a). Therefore, each brother brought an offering that represented his daily endeavors. God considered both offerings, seeing with favor "Abel and his offering" (v. 4b). Many scholars have tried to explain why God preferred the younger brother's offering. We could summarize some of these theories, trying to defend God in the process. However, God does not need to be defended. The Bible simply states that one offering was pleasing to God and that the other was not, without further explanation.

Cain reacted with much pain to God's ruling. We should note that the Bible describes his reaction in terms that remind us of a depressive state: "So Cain was very angry, and his countenance fell" (v. 5b). Nonetheless, it would be a mistake to "psychologize" the text. Cain did not react violently because he needed Prozac or because he suffered from "bipolar disorder."

On the contrary, Cain reacted with pain because he understood that God's decision had dishonored him.

In biblical times, the firstborn son had more authority and rights that the rest of the siblings. He inherited a "double portion," that is, twice as much money and properties than the rest. During the father's absence, he acted as head of the household. After the father's death, he became the leader of the clan.

The elder son also had to take over the spiritual leadership of the family. The head of the household led family devotions, prayed for the family members, and granted divine blessing upon them. According to these traditions, Cain was the heir of the spiritual leadership of his family, not Abel. The rejection of his sacrifice thus became an offense, an affront, a dishonorable act. It is precisely this false sense of honor that moves Cain to murder his brother. His honor, blemished by God's rejection, needs to be restored. He needs to avenge the offense motivated by his brother's offering.

God, who sees Cain's heart, calls him to change his heart. God calls him to act with justice, if he wants to be honored. God warns him that "sin is lurking at the door" (v. 7b), ready to take control of his life. However, Cain does not heed God's warning. On the contrary, thirsty for vengeance, he goes looking for his brother. He dupes Abel, takes him to a field, and murders him (v. 8).

God goes searching for the fratricidal brother, demanding to know Abel's whereabouts, therefore giving Cain an opportunity to confess his sin. On his part, Cain answers with scorn, uttering one of the most cynical phrases in all of scripture: "I do not know; am I my brother's keeper?" (v. 9). Offended by Cain's cynical fib, God confronts Cain, saying: "What have you done? Listen; your brother's blood is crying out to me from the ground!" (v. 10).

Listen, the blood of our brothers and sisters is crying to God from Ground Zero!

The tragedy endured on September 11 is a sad example of the consequences of sin that, hidden behind a door, are ready to destroy us. The attack on the twin towers of the World Trade Center will be remembered as an evil and cowardly act. The assassination of thousands of innocent victims, the wounds inflicted on thousands of workers and commuters, and the terror sowed in the inhabitants of this great city are sinful acts, acts that God definitely repudiates and rejects.

From the very moment of the first plane crash, many have asked: "How can God allow this awful tragedy to happen?" It must be clear that God is not responsible for human evil acts.

- God did not guide the murderers, nor did God help them to commit murder.
- God did not punish those who died on the planes, nor the ones who disappeared when the buildings collapsed.
- God takes no pleasure in human wickedness.

These murderous acts demonstrate that in our world there are people who dedicate their lives to practice sin, serve evil, and be agents of death.

- God rejects the forces of death and battles against those who serve them.
- God wills that humanity enjoy life at its fullest, taking pleasure in the goodness of creation, and blessing others with happiness.
- The God revealed through the life and death of Jesus Christ does not kill anybody; the God of Life is not a murderer.

The deaths of Jos… D. Sánchez, Esmerlin Salcedo, Eliezer Jim…nez, John Robert Cruz, and others related to our Hispanic Disciples congregations are the consequence of human sin, not of God's will. They are the consequence of a savage act of vengeance perpetrated by a gang of men who, like Cain, were in search of an elusive sense of honor.

"Vengeance?" we may ask. "Why did they want vengeance?" They wanted to avenge the British hegemony over the Arab countries; the deaths of thousands of Palestinians during the last fifty-three years; the murder of hundreds of Lebanese civilians in the 1980s; the loss of over a quarter million Iraqi soldiers; and the way in which the United States recruited, trained, and financed the Afghan guerrillas in order to fight the Soviet armies, only to abandon them in the process.

The September 11 murderers thought that the assassination of thousands of innocent victims would avenge the deaths of their ancestors, relatives, and friends. Just as with Cain, a false sense of honor led them to murder.

Our country must remember the lesson of this biblical text, avoiding desires of vengeance motivated by a mistaken sense of honor. Otherwise, our acts of vengeance will only cause further tragedy in the Arab and Islamic countries, which, in their turn, will be avenged by future generations. We need to do everything possible to avoid this circle of death and vengeance.

I believe that we must learn from both the biblical text and the sad experience of September 11. Vengeance is an instrument of sin that we must reject. We must, then, pray to God asking to be freed from any feelings of vengeance. *Let us learn, then, that murder is never justified, even when it is committed for honor's sake.*

In spite of my words, many may still ask: "Where was God when the Twin Towers were collapsing?" I do not know. I cannot give the definitive answer to such a question. I can only share with you my hunch that the key to the answer from a Christian perspective lies at the foot of the cross. Jesus also died in a tragic manner, at the hands of a religious "elite" willing to punish the "blasphemer," that is, the preacher who had dishonored their religion. Jesus died at the hands of a military machine willing to punish the subversive preacher who, having declared himself "king of the Jews," had dishonored the Roman emperor.

I am convinced that on September 11, Jesus was, once again, dying tragically on the cross.

I am convinced that, on that day, Jesus was buried under a pile of steel and concrete.

And I am convinced that those who die with Jesus Christ will be raised with him.

The Mystery of Grace

Thomas J. Reese, S.J.

Thomas Reese is editor-in-chief of the Jesuit magazine *America*. This homily was preached at St. Ignatius Loyola Church in Manhattan, New York City, on Sunday, September 16, 2001.

First reading: Exodus 32:7–11, 13–14

The first reading is from the book of Exodus. In the section we read today, Yahweh has already led the Hebrews out of slavery in Egypt and the people are camped at the foot of Mt. Sinai. They are getting impatient because Moses has been up on the mountain for forty days receiving instructions from the Lord. The people build for themselves idols and begin to worship them. As our reading begins, God is informing Moses of what is going on.

Second reading: 1 Timothy 1:12–17

The second reading today is from the First Letter to Timothy. We will be hearing from this letter for the rest of September, and then next month we will be reading from the Second Letter to Timothy. The actual author of these letters is probably a follower of Paul rather than Paul himself. In ancient times it was not unusual for the disciple of a great leader to write using the leader's name. In any case, the writer uses Paul's sinfulness and conversion as an example of God's mercy and grace.

Gospel: Luke 15:1–32

Faced with the enormity of suffering and evil that we have seen this past week, it is impossible to find words that are adequate to comprehend it. If you have come here today hoping to find answers to why this tragedy has occurred, I am afraid that you will be disappointed. I have no answers. In the face of such disaster, silence and prayer are probably the only adequate responses.

Last week, I had to write an editorial on the terrorist attack. I won't repeat my policy analysis and recommendations here; this is not the place for that. I would simply repeat the words of Pope John Paul with which I concluded my editorial: "This was a dark day in the history of humanity. But even if the forces of darkness appear to prevail, those who believe in God know that evil and death do not have the final say."

The problem of evil has been examined since at least the time of Job, and no one has come up with an adequate answer. If God is all-powerful, how can such tragedies be permitted to occur? Perhaps our mistake is in thinking that God is all-powerful. Perhaps creation limited God in ways we do not understand. Certainly, the God portrayed by Jesus was not all-powerful—he was tortured and crucified. He hangs on the cross in solidarity with all those who have suffered unjustly. His resurrection shows that, in the words of John Paul, "Evil and death do not have the final say."

But besides the problem of evil, there is also the mystery of love. In nature, the struggle for life involves the survival of the fittest. The strong prey upon the weak. Here we are surprised by altruism and love when the strong sacrifice themselves for the weak. The believer is faced with trying to explain the problem of evil; the unbeliever is faced with trying to explain the mystery of love.

The gospel reading today portrays God not as a vengeful God, not as a punishing God, but as a God who searches for sinners so that he can save them. In the first parable, Jesus describes a shepherd who searches for his lost sheep in the desert. When he finds it, he does not punish it for getting lost, but puts it on his shoulders and brings it home with great joy. Likewise, Jesus portrays God as a woman searching for her lost coin. She sweeps the house, lights a lamp. She spends more time and energy searching for her coin than it is probably worth.

If Jesus were with us today, he would tell another parable. He would tell us how God is like a rescue worker who comes all the way up from Florida to spend his vacation time helping out at Ground Zero. God is like a fireman who runs into a burning building, risking his life to save another. God is like the rescue workers who worked nonstop for hours trying to find victims who could be rescued. When horrible tragedies like the World Trade Center attack occur, we are confronted with the enormity of evil and sin, but we are also surprised by grace. Grace is at work after the attack even more than sin was at work before the attack.

The second reading gives us another example of the mystery of grace. Paul was a blasphemer, a persecutor of Christians, and a man of great arrogance. But the Lord grants him mercy in overflowing measure. Not only is he forgiven, he is transformed. He is made an apostle filled with faith and love in Christ Jesus.

A few years ago, a similar transformation occurred in an Italian prison where former members of the Red Brigade, with the help of prison chaplains, repented of their crimes and became pacifists. It is hard for us to believe that such conversion is possible when faced with such evil.

As we as a nation prepare to respond to these terrorist crimes, we must seek justice, but not vengeance. We must not imitate our attackers, who demonize ethnic or religious groups. We must not kill civilians when trying to punish terrorists.

We are faced with a long and grim struggle ahead as we comfort those left bhind, rebuild our city, and struggle to build a world of justice and peace. As we continue this eucharist, we join Jesus the suffering servant, in seeking comfort from a loving God who searches through the rubble for his loved ones.

How Will We Find Our Way Home Now?

Mary Forell-Davis

The Rev. Mary Forell-Davis is pastor of St. Matthew Lutheran Church in Hoboken, New Jersey, where this sermon was preached on Sunday, September 23, 2001.

An editorial appeared in Friday's *New York Times* written by a resident of Battery Park City. Until September 11, Battery Park City was a vibrant new community located next to the World Trade Center. Now it is a ghost town, its residents missing, evacuated, and scattered. The author describes in his letter being one of the first residents of that community when the first residential tower went up, and how the community grew and developed and became home to many families, complete with parks and playgrounds. He describes how parents in this community would tell their children, if they ever got lost, simply to look for the twin towers and then they could find their way home.

Now the towers are gone, and many of the residents who worked in the WTC are missing. This week, one of the children who lived in Battery Park asked his mother: "How will I find my way home now?"

How will I find my way home now?

The disaster has left us all disoriented as well as grieving. What is security in an age of terror? What is safe to do and what is not? Should I take that business trip or beg off? Where are we going? What happened to the familiar contour of our skyline? How will we find our way home now?

Today the immediate demands of the disaster continue. Exhausted rescue workers keep on sifting through rubble for clues and remains. Frantic relatives and friends here and abroad persist in trying to locate loved ones. Congregations continue to try to help, offering prayer and conversation, vigils and memorials, shelter and concern.

But even as these demands recede and the mammoth job of rebuilding NYC begins, you and I, as Christian believers, will have a continuing critical message to proclaim in the days and the nights to come. This message that we have been given has to do with how to help people find their way home.

One part of this message concerns priorities. On Tuesday morning, when the first plane hit the first tower, one man who was in his office reported how difficult it was for people to put down their telephones, leave their desks, and get out. Precious minutes passed while his coworkers lingered on the phones, finished sales calls, tidied the papers on their desks, or searched for their possessions. This man, who had served in the armed forces and had a greater sense of the urgency of escaping the damaged building, finally yelled at his coworkers, rounded them up, and demanded that they drop everything and leave with him. He led them to safety.

I read an interview with another person who had considered staying in the office when it was evacuated in order to keep it secure. When he got home to his family, he could not believe that he had even considered making such a choice.

When the Board of the Hoboken Shelter for the Homeless met on Thursday, each person's entrance was greeted with joy and relief. People whose presence I normally take for granted I, right now, recognize as infinitely precious to me.

The events of September 11 have challenged our priorities. And the church can help us to redefine those priorities. When Jesus approached Matthew, who was seated at the tax booth, and said, "Follow me," Matthew did not finish up his transactions, or linger over his pile of money. Matthew up and left what he was doing to follow Jesus.

As Doug so eloquently said last week, neither the meaning of our lives nor our safety can be found in our financial institutions but rather in our relationships with God and with one another. It is through these relationships that we will find our way home.

A second message that the church has to deliver to those who are lost is to help discover the presence of God in the midst of disaster. People who follow Jesus follow a leader whose faithfulness to God led him to a cruel death—and beyond.

One child from the Hoboken Charter School drew a picture of the twin towers with a superman-like figure, with arm outstretched, halting the airplane heading for the tower. To me this child's powerful drawing represents our deep wish that God had prevented this disaster.

We don't understand the mind of God; but we do know that the promises of God include the promise to be with us in the midst of whatever happens to us. As St. Paul put it:

> For I am convinced that neither death, nor life, nor angels, nor rulers, nor things present, nor things to come, nor powers, nor height, nor depth, nor anything else in all creation, will be able to separate us from the love of God in Christ Jesus our Lord. (Romans 8:38–39)

God is present in tragedy—in our grief and in our longing. God is present in the mourning of those who have lost people they love and in the struggles of those who have lost their homes and their jobs. God is with us in the joy of our reunions and in the sorrow of our separations. How will we find our way home now? God will take us by the hand and lead us home.

A third message that we have been given to deliver is a message to the grieving. Many have died in this disaster. The numbers of missing and confirmed dead are staggering and climb relentlessly each day. Still more are likely to die in the armed conflict ahead. Some bodies have been recovered, but many others never will be. Young lives were interrupted. Wonderful, caring people left behind bereft children, spouses, parents, and friends. Courageous firefighters, police officers, and rescue workers marched to their deaths to save others. Parents and spouses, coworkers and beloved friends are gone.

Our message to the grieving is that while we can no longer touch or see or hear our loved ones, we know that they are in God's loving embrace. We know that they are still part of God's plan, because God is the God of the living and the dead. Those who were lost have already been found.

Our gift to the grieving is to help them to commend those who have died into God's care. Because even though they are beyond our reach, we know that they are in God's loving embrace. God has led them to their eternal home.

A fourth message that we have been given to deliver may not be such a popular one right now, but nevertheless it is ours to proclaim, and it is good news. This message is that the God we worship is the God of the entire universe. So, even as we join our neighbors in the prayer "God bless America," as Christians we are compelled to pray with equal fervor, "God bless Afghanistan" and "God bless Iraq." Christians continually pray for God to bless all of God's children and every nation under heaven.

We ask for God's consoling presence with our loved ones. But we also ask God to be with the families of the terrorists who died in committing these terrible acts of violence. In this way, Christians can serve as a web of connection and caring that connects the entire globe. We proclaim a message of love so powerful that it overcomes all differences.

How will we find our way home now? Not by looking for the twin towers, and not even by rebuilding them, but we will find our way home by orienting ourselves by the cross of Christ, "towering over the wrecks of time." And if we use the cross and the love of Christ to guide us, we will not only find our way home, but lead others to safety as well.

The peace of God, which surpasses all human understanding, keep our hearts and our minds in Christ Jesus. Amen.

A Day of Terror

Adam Hamilton

Adam Hamilton is founding pastor of the United Methodist Church of the Resurrection, Leawood, Kansas. He preached this sermon to his congregation in six different services on Saturday and Sunday, September 15 and 16, 2001.

Tuesday morning, September 11, 2001, is a day that will be etched in our minds for the rest of our lives.

On that day I was awakened by one of our staff, who said, "Adam, please turn on the television set." I said, "Why? What is it?" and the person said, "Just turn it on." I turned on the television set to see that there had been an explosion in one of the towers at the World Trade Center. Someone thought that perhaps an airplane had crashed into the building, that some terrible accident had taken place, and while I sat there watching the television set as many of you did, I watched as a commercial jet plane crashed into the second of the two World Trade Center towers.

We have, of course, seen this image over and over and over again. I sat glued to the television set for a period of time—stunned, numb, unable really to comprehend what was just taking place—when a journalist broke in and said they were at the Pentagon and that there had been an explosion there. Shortly after that, we discovered that another airplane had, in fact, crashed into the Pentagon. Not much time went by before there was an airplane that had turned around over Cleveland, was heading back toward Washington, D.C., and then crashed near Pittsburgh. By the time I came over here to the church, I arrived just in time to watch the first Trade Center building collapse under its own weight, and then the second.

All day sitting and watching, thoughts of Armageddon running through my mind, I tried to pray; but every time I tried to pray, I found I just started crying. We had a prayer service here at 10:15 a.m. with the staff and those in Disciples Bible study and later on that night another prayer service. The day was spent glued to the television set, craving information, wanting to know more about what was happening, and why and how this could take place. Questions were flooding my mind, as with many of you, and then throughout the days after, trying to understand, trying to make sense of this—questions and questions and more questions. Tonight we are going to try to reflect on four of those questions through the lens of our Christian faith to allow the gospel to shed some light on these questions that plague our minds.

The first is, Why did this happen? Why *did* this happen? Among those many questions that were running through our minds, perhaps this was the most important one on that first day. As some of us stood by the television set in the narthex watching as one of the Trade Center towers collapsed, a woman with tears streaming down her face asked the question this way: "Why do they hate us so much?" Why do they hate us so much? This is a very, very important question. If we do not take the time to answer this question, to understand the motivation behind those who are doing these things, we stand in the position of potentially making dreadful mistakes in how we respond.

There was a little boy who was playing in his family's garage. His father had a shop in the garage. There were sawdust and scraps of wood, and the boy was playing with matches. As he threw one match to the ground, the sawdust caught on fire. It would not have burned the house down; it was just a small pile of sawdust. It would have eventually burned itself out. But the boy got scared and ran to his father's workbench. There he found a peanut butter jar with clear fluid in it. Thinking it was water, he ran to the flames and he poured the paint thinner all over the flames and, of course, it exploded with fire. This is what I fear we are about to do as a country if we do not understand what it is that's taking place and why these people are doing what they are doing.

Now, we'll offer a unique perspective on that, perhaps one that you haven't had on the news or heard very much of, but one that came as I began to study this and tried to understand what was taking place. There were certain elements that began to fit together. I could be entirely wrong about this, but I think that it may very well be that this is close to the truth or at least helpful in putting these pieces of the puzzle together. We have been trying to analyze who it was that might be behind this and, though he denies it, the primary suspect is one Osama bin Laden.

Perhaps you have been reading and studying about him this week. Beginning on Tuesday afternoon, I began trying to read everything I could about this man, trying to understand why he did what he did. Now it would be very easy for us to say that he is simply insane, he is absolutely, utterly mad. By all accounts from people who have met with him, he is not insane. So one wonders, Why? Why a man in the mountains of Afghanistan would be concerned about the United States. Why is he intent on destroying us? And, then, there were nineteen young men who died in this act who believed that whatever it was they were doing was so important that they were willing to give their lives for it. Why? Now if they were all mad, we could dismiss this but, by all accounts, they were not insane either. Why? Why did they do this?

For Osama bin Laden, if you study his interviews, if you listen to the people who are closest to him, it seems as if what is at stake for this man is the very future of Islam. He and his followers and the Taliban of Afghanistan, who are the party most closely aligned with his thinking and also happen to be the ruling party of Afghanistan—these folks seem to believe that America is a threat to their faith. We've got to understand this. As Americans, we don't often have a sense of history, of what went on centuries before us. These people remember.

As you listen to Osama bin Laden it seems that he is looking at the events of the last fifty or sixty years in the Middle East through the lens of the Crusades. The Crusades. You remember them from history class. The eleventh through thirteenth centuries—the darkest point in Christian history. I'll remind you that in the mid-600s during the lifetime of Muhammad, Muslims began to take control of the Holy Land, and from the mid-600s until the eleventh century Muslims controlled that piece of ground. It was in the eleventh century that the kings in Christian Western Europe launched a crusade to oust the infidels from the Holy Land and to take it back for Jesus Christ. The armies from Western Europe marched on the Holy Land, and you remember they initially met with victory. They would send reports back to the king saying that the blood of the infidels flowed through the streets of Jerusalem as high as the bridles of their horses. They were very proud of this, and they took back this land as a gift to Jesus. And then the counterattacks came. For two hundred years it went back and forth from the hands of Western European Christians and the hands of Muslims until, finally in the thirteenth century, Christians were ousted altogether and for good.

From the 1200s until 1947 Muslims controlled the Holy Land. In 1947, under a decree of the United Nations, much of the land was set aside to form the State of Israel. For persons who process information the way bin Laden does, the "crusaders" are back, they have forged an alliance with the Jews, and in one fell swoop, with the United Nations decree, they took back that land. They have held it against the Muslims, who have tried to take it back from them, because of the power and influence of the United States of America. Listen to what Osama bin Laden says in 1999 in an interview conducted with Jamal Ismail in Afghanistan. I want you to hear carefully what he says: "There was an attack on the countries of Islam especially on the holy shrines and on the Al Aqsa Mosque." The attack he's describing is in 1947 when Palestine was taken, at least portions of it, and turned into the State of Israel. The Al Aqsa Mosque is the mosque adjacent to the Dome of the Rock, which is built on the former site of the Temple in Jerusalem. It is the third holiest shrine in Islam. Then the aggression continued with, as bin Laden puts it, "The Crusader-Jewish alliance led by the United States and Israel. Now, they have taken the country of the two holy mosques." The country of the two holy mosques is Saudi Arabia, and the two holy mosques are located in Mecca and Medina. These are the two holiest sites for Islam.

So, how did he come to believe that we had taken that land? Osama bin Laden did not begin to focus his attention on the United States until the early 1990s, when American troops were first stationed on Saudi soil. Now listen carefully. These persons look at the United States and see us as a "Christian nation." In Afghanistan they are an Islamic nation. Most of the nations in that region are Islamic nations. You understand yourselves to be a nation of Christians. Seventy percent of us are Christians in America. They look at us and see the most Christian nation in the world. And now, not only have the crusaders taken back the Holy Land, but the crusaders' troops are stationed on Saudi soil in the heart of the holiest place to the Muslim faith. You are the Crusader alliance.

This idea becomes more interesting when we understand that Osama bin Laden's father was awarded the contract as the protector and restorer of the three holy shrines for Islam. He restored the Dome of the Rock in Jerusalem. He restored and rebuilt and built and added on to Mecca and Medina. These three holy sites the bin Laden family is responsible for taking care of, maintaining, and restoring. And you, you are the "infidels." You are the unfaithful, those who are not following Allah in the true way, and you are on their soil. Not only are you on their soil, stationed in Saudi Arabia, but you have also been involved in dropping bombs on Iraq. You have been involved in Iran; you have been involved in Egypt and have troops there. You have been involved in Kuwait. In almost every Muslim country, your troops are somehow involved. Our troops are involved from their perspective, this skewed sort of twisted perspective—and you are a threat to their faith. They believe that they are waging a defensive war against the offensive crusaders.

Perhaps you were watching this week on the news when they were showing film clips of Osama bin Laden's training camp. In this training camp, if you looked very carefully, they were training terrorists for this war, this defensive war protecting Islam and the future of Islam. Terrorist commandos practiced storming a room and dummies that were set up in the room represented the enemies of Osama bin Laden. Did you notice what was draped across their chests? It was not a United States flag. It was a cross, giant crosses draped across their necks.

If you read the article yesterday in the *Kansas City Star* about the Taliban, the Taliban stated that they are anticipating our bombs coming on Afghanistan. But did you read carefully what they said in the article? They said, "We will die, we are willing to fight to the death to preserve and protect our Muslim faith." It's important that you understand this, because the response that America makes could very well play right into that fear that we are trying to take away their faith, to snuff out Islam or at least to push them back and back and back, to control what is happening in that part of the world. You are the Crusaders. You are the infidels.

It's important also to understand that Osama bin Laden does not represent the Islamic faith. He is to the Islamic faith what the Ku Klux Klan is to Christianity. None of us in this room would say that the Ku Klux Klan is authentic Christianity. Most Muslims around the world would say that what Osama bin Laden preaches is not authentic Islam, and they would distance themselves from him. We need to remember that.

You, as Christians in this community, need to get this word out. We Americans have a difficult time telling the difference between someone from India and an Arab. We don't know the difference between Hinduism, which is what the Indians preach and practice, and Islam, which is what many in the Arab nations practice. An Indian family, who are Hindus, were walking down their own street in their own neighborhood while their neighbors rolled down their windows, honked their horns, and hurled obscenities at them. This is in our neighborhood, this is in the Blue Valley community. If you are not the folks who are going to understand and stand up for what's right here, I do not know who will. This is about our Christian witness. This is about what we believe and the kind of nation we say we are. It is very important that we are clear about this: Even those who are Muslims in our country would distance themselves from this.

Now even given the distorted perspective that bin Laden and his followers have on American intentions in the Middle East, his actions are a reflection of his picture of God. It's important that you understand this as well, that he has a picture of a god who is willing to use force in order to accomplish his purposes, who is willing to have clerics kill other people in what is called a *jihad* or a holy war. So his picture is a god of judgment, and a god of wrath, a god who is willing to fight and kill even innocent people in order to accomplish his ends. That is his picture of God, and so his activities are consistent with his faith.

Let me ask you this, What is your picture of God? What does God look like to you? We who are Christians believe that God looks very much like Jesus Christ. That God put on human flesh and walked among us as a man to show us what he is like, to teach us the truth, to show us what it means to be authentically human. So Jesus is our picture of God: Jesus, who takes the children on his lap; Jesus, who welcomes the Gentiles; Jesus, who says that we are to forgive as the Lord has forgiven us. Jesus, who teaches us to love our enemies and pray for those who persecute us; Jesus, who when he was dying on the cross said to those who were watching and to God, "Father, forgive them for they do not know what they are doing." That is the picture of God that you as Christians espouse and that is very, very, very different from the picture of God that Osama bin Laden espouses.

And that takes us to our next question. This week we have been experiencing corporate grief in our country. We watched what happened on television; it was the unthinkable, and as we continued to watch it and play it over and over and over again, inside we began to experience that common shared grief. Now those who have lost loved ones in New York or Washington, D.C., or outside of Pittsburgh will experience this grief over the next year or two. For the rest of us it will be telescoped down into a very short period of time.

Dr. Elizabeth Kübler-Ross mentions five stages of grief that people typically go through during periods like this. The first is denial and isolation. The second is anger and the desire for vengeance. The third is bargaining. The fourth is depression, and the fifth is acceptance. Where is America today in these five stages? For most of us, we have moved beyond stage one and are in stage two, which is anger and a desire for vengeance or revenge. I must admit that this week while I was watching this over and over and over again, there were times that I felt such hate and I was so angry and I wanted so much for the wrath of the United States to be poured out on whoever had done this. I wasn't really concerned about being discriminate in pouring out that wrath. Somebody needed to see what happens when you mess with the United States of America. I felt that, and maybe you did too.

The Bible teaches us that there are times that we will feel that, even as faithful Christians. Psalm 137 was written to teach us that very thing. The writer of Psalm 137 has watched the destruction of Jerusalem. Their homes had been destroyed, friends were killed, their loved ones were raped, their homes and their property had been pillaged, they watched the Temple of God razed to the ground, and then they were carried away as slaves to Babylon. In Babylon, the writer penned these words that have stood out to many as perplexing within the Bible, as not being fitting and appropriate for the Bible. We have been embarrassed by them and wished they weren't there and, yet, at times like this we understand.

> Remember, O LORD, against the Edomites the day of Jerusalem's fall, how they said, "Tear it down! Tear it down! Down to its foundations!" O daughter Babylon, you devastator! Happy shall they be who pay you back what you have done to us! Happy shall they be who take your little ones and dash them against the rock! (Psalm 137:7–9)

A prayer for someone to take someone else's children and dash them against the stones? In the Bible? This prayer is found in the scriptures to let us know that it is okay to be extremely angry and to want vengeance in the midst of our pain. But we are not meant to stay at Psalm 137. We are allowed to feel it. God understands. And then we are to move beyond Psalm 137 and the desire for vengeance and retribution. During times like this when we are going through grief and we've experienced tragedy, the world seems to be very unsafe. Some of you are going to board airplanes this week, and you're going to think two or three times—and so will your family members—about that.

My first experience in losing people that I really care about happened in my freshman year of college. Two of my best friends were killed in an accident, and I remember every day after that when LaVon was even five minutes late getting home from work I was terrified that she had been in an accident, that something terrible had happened to her. I needed her to call me. That was before cell phones. I was so worried because my world had been turned upside down. I thought people were safe, the people I loved were safe, and now they weren't and I didn't know what to think about that. It took me months and months to finally get to the place where I wasn't afraid when she was late getting home from work. That will be the case for many of you.

This week someone was interviewed on National Public Radio and they were being asked about the economic impact of this tragedy. One woman was asked, "What impact will this have on you and the decisions you're making?" She said, "I had planned on buying a new sport utility vehicle this coming week, and now I'm postponing that. I'm not going to be doing that because today the future seems so uncertain." Pastor Rob Winger heard that and said, "Adam, when was the future ever certain?" The future is not certain. There is no certainty. We are going to do everything we can to beef up security at our airports, and this kind of incident will probably never happen again quite like this. No matter how many police and military personnel you put at the airports, and we need to take measures there, that will not buy you security. No matter how strong our military might be in America, no matter that you live in the heartland of the country, that will not gain you security, because our security cannot be found in our military might or security measures.

You have installed a burglar alarm in your house, perhaps, but you're also aware that if somebody really wants to break in, they will find a way around that. If someone wants to hurt America, if they want to terrorize us, they'll find another way. So where is your security? The only real security we have comes from our faith in Jesus Christ. That's it. On Tuesday morning when these folks walked out of their homes, kissed their children good-bye, boarded their airplanes, and went into their offices, there was no other security except that they might have known that they belonged to Jesus Christ and He belonged to them. That no matter what happened in their lives, somehow God would make it okay. That they would either be in His presence for all eternity, or He would save them and deliver them. That whatever evil takes place in some peoples' hearts, He would bend it and force it to bring about good for other people, because they belonged to Him and He belonged to them.

Where is your security? Today, at 3:50 p.m., somebody called saying there was a bomb at the Church of the Resurrection. For those of you who walked in late, the building was swept by police officers and the fire department, and they believe that was a hoax. But let me ask you this question: If that happened tonight in our worship service, is it well with your soul? Are you ready? Do you have security in Jesus Christ? We never know when that day comes.

There is a third question that we ask. This is a question being asked by a teenager as she was being interviewed by CNN when one of her parents was missing in one of the World Trade Center towers. She asked, "What kind of God lets things like this happen?" This week I had the opportunity to speak on channel 9 and on one of the radio stations here in Kansas City, and each time the interviewer would ask me this: "Where was God on Tuesday morning?" Where was God on Tuesday morning? For those of you who have been a part of Church of the Resurrection for a long time, you've heard the answer to that. We preach it two or three times a year, but for those of you who may be new, I'll share with you a thumbnail sketch of the answer to this fundamental question.

The answer to the question of the problem of evil in our world begins and is found on the opening pages in your Bible. It's found in the story of Adam and Eve—the creation story. This is a story meant not to teach us biology and our human origins; it's meant to teach us about who we are as human beings, about our spirit, about our soul, and why we are the way we are.

In this story, God creates human beings to be different from all the other creatures on this planet. Every other creature follows its instincts. It doesn't have a soul as you have a soul. You were created in the image of God. That doesn't mean you look like God physically, it means that inside you have the characteristics of God. You are spirit beings. It means that you have the capacity to love and to think and to reason and to transcend yourself and to reach out to God and to understand God and to understand God's glory. But it also means that God has given you the wonderful and terrifying possibility of human freedom. Freedom. In that story, God places Adam and Eve in the garden and then He places a tree there. You remember the tree, the tree of the knowledge of good and evil. God says to Adam and Eve, "Now, listen, whatever you do, don't eat the fruit from this tree, for in the day that you eat of it, you will unleash some very bad things on this world. You will die on that day." Haven't you often wondered why God put the tree there to begin with? If it was going to have that potential devastation, if it was going to be that tempting to Adam and Eve so that they would go ahead and eat the fruit, as you know that they did, why did God put the tree there anyway? It didn't have to be in the garden. It could have been outside the garden. It didn't even have to be revealed to them.

The reason God put the tree there is that it stands for something much bigger. It is archetypal. It stands for our freedom to choose to follow God or reject God. And God has given you that freedom as well. The entire Bible is the story of human freedom and of people either choosing to follow God and be faithful or to reject God and turn away. Now, if God had given us no help and no direction, given us freedom and nothing else, we would be right to call God a monster. But that isn't how it works. That would be something akin to you giving your sixteen-year-old children the keys to the car having never given them driver's education, never having taught them how to drive, just giving them the keys and saying, "Go ahead and drive." They would be bound to hurt themselves and someone else. You would be culpable for that, but you would never do that.

Likewise, God does not let us loose on this world with our freedom. Instead He gave us the law and said, "Now, listen! This is how I want you to live—the Ten Commandments and the rest of the law—and if you live in this way, you'll prosper and you'll have life. Enjoy. But if you don't, devastating things will happen." Then when the people disobeyed the law, He sent the prophets, who said, "Please! Follow God's commands because you are in terrible danger of hurting yourselves and other people. Please follow His commands and ordinances." When the people refused, He sent his son. God clothed himself with human flesh and came and walked among us to show us what it means to be authentically human and to live our lives following after His pattern to redeem us from the consequences of our sin. He then poured out his Holy Spirit on us so that His spirit might bear witness of how we should live.

Then He gave us the gift of the church and then gave us the Bible. All of these things are meant to be our guides. God has said, "This is how you should live, and if you live in this way, you will prosper." The reality is that if the whole world followed God's commands and ordinances, we wouldn't be having this conversation. God has given us the tremendous gift of freedom, this gift of freedom we wouldn't want taken away. For you and me, as Americans, this is our most treasured possession. We would die for freedom. We would sooner die than live without it.

But God has done something more than that, knowing what would happen with our freedom. God has also promised to be with us when others wreak havoc as the consequence of their freedom. You say, "Where was Jesus on Tuesday morning at 8:48 a.m.?" I think he was huddled in the back of a commercial jetliner with people who were about to die. I think at 9:48 a.m., Jesus was standing in the fiery furnace as he had with Shadrach, Meshach, and Abednego thousands of years before. I think Jesus was prompting and working through the hands of those firefighters and those police officers who were giving their lives to try to save other people. I think He was prompting the hearts of thousands upon thousands of people to try to come and help and deliver them. I think He stood on the other side of that river that every one of us will cross one day and said to those who perished, "Welcome home. It's okay now. You're in my hands."

It isn't only the promise of eternal life that we have, of course. It is this confidence that God is ultimately in control of history, that God's purposes cannot ultimately be thwarted, though evil may seem to succeed for a season. Here is what God always does. God forces that evil that others meant to destroy us with, He forces it to be used to accomplish His purposes. What does that look like? Well, you can imagine the joy and the delight of the devil at the destruction and pain that was wrought this last week. And Osama bin Laden, who was watching as, in a picture perfect way, the timing of this worked out so that we could watch it in horror on television, how he hoped that people would rise up and fight against that enemy—the infidels—America. But what did God do through that? God solidified a nation so that thousands of people in New York City, who the day before might have walked by people who were hurting, are suddenly pouring out their lives to help everyone else. He brought an entire nation of people to its knees in this country.

What has God done? Well, look around the world and see what has happened as a result of this. It wasn't the evil that Osama bin Laden wished but, instead, look at the nations of the world and how they have responded. We received an e-mail this week from Moscow where thousands upon thousands of Russians stood outside the U.S. Embassy and laid flowers at the embassy gates and carried American flags, even army officers laying down their hats on the pile of flowers. A reporter said, "I wish you could have seen it. The people were weeping and weeping and weeping for America." These people, our former enemy, the very next day observed a moment of prayer across the country; a former atheist state asking the entire country to pray for America. Or of all things, in Iran, 60,000 people in attendance at a World Cup soccer game who stopped—in Iran—to pray for America and observe a moment of silence in shared pain for our shared humanity. Or 200,000 people outside the remains of the Berlin Wall who were marching and chanting and praying and weeping for America. Can't you hear the devil in the throes of pain as he sees what was meant for evil, but in God's hands is turned once more into something that accomplishes His purposes?

There is yet one thing that needs to be said about this. Yesterday I opened up the newspaper to see that some of my fellow colleagues in the ministry had determined that perhaps God had allowed this to happen as an act of judgment on America for our going easy on the perceived socials sins that they were speaking of, that perhaps we deserved what we got. We had it coming because America needed to repent and God wanted to teach us a lesson through this. So God lifted His hedge of protection and allowed this evil thing to take place. In pulpits across America that will be preached in certain churches today. Listen very, very carefully. I have a question for you: If you wanted to teach your child something, would you kill her best friend to teach her that? Would you take your child and slam him into the building as hard as you could and allow glass to cut him up into pieces in order to bring him to a place of repentance? Would you crush your children in order to make sure that they had a chance to know your will? If you would not do this as human parents, how could we think that God, who is our heavenly Father, could act in this way? Yes, God wants us to learn something from all of this. Yes, God would have us fall on our knees as a result of this. But God does not do this thing to us so that He can teach us.

Evil people did this evil thing. We have much we can learn from it, and there are many ways we can come to the Lord as a result of it; but God did not do this to teach you a lesson or to bring America to repent for our social sins. This is not how the God that was manifested in Jesus Christ operates. What is your picture of God, I ask you again? I understand where these pastors are coming from. One of the phases of grief is that you begin to blame yourself for things. So maybe we are blaming ourselves for things that other people have done wrong.

Several years ago, in the face of a tragedy that took place at that time, one man said to me, "Look. Look at this tragedy. This proves, doesn't it, that there is no God. How could there be a God if something like this happens?" I said, "It's interesting that you should say that, because you look at this tragedy and say that's proof there is no God, and I look at this tragedy and say that's proof that there must be a God."

He said, "What do you mean?"

I said, "Okay. Here. We have the same tragedy—both of us. If you take God out of the picture, the tragedy does not go away. The tragedy is there whether God is in the picture or not. But listen: Here is what you have in the face of that tragedy. You have hopelessness, despair, and pain. Here's what I have. I have a framework for understanding, through the truth of God's Word, why people are the way they are or why they do the things they do and why that is not God's plan. And I have more than that. I have the confidence that those people that died in this tragedy belong to Jesus Christ, and they are in his arms, and some day their loved ones will see them again, and there was hope for them beyond this life. This is not the end for them, that their lives were snuffed short and nothing more. I have more than that. I have the power of the Holy Spirit, who prompts the hearts of people who are Christians—God's people—to come and sacrifice for these folks and stand by them. I have more than *that* because when I fall on my knees, and I weep, and I become quiet, there is someone I become quieted before who bears me up. But I have more than *that*. There is a God who is healing those who are surrounding the situation. I have more than *that*, because God is able to take this thing that you see as only hopeless and tragic and bend it to accomplish His good and bring good out of the evil you have seen. I have hope, and you have nothing."

That leads us to the last question: How does a Christian nation respond? I understand that we are not a Christian nation but, rather, a nation of Christians. For the people in the Middle East you are a Christian nation. For Osama bin Laden you are the Crusaders. How will you respond? We wish we could go back and change the crusades. We are embarrassed for that period of time where our picture of God in the eleventh through the thirteenth centuries said that we kill in the name of God to honor Jesus Christ. We wish we could change that. How do we respond? Our president is a Christian, a United Methodist. Most of our members of Congress are Christians. Most of the Joint Chiefs of Staff are Christians. Most of the Cabinet members are Christians. How do we respond? How do we decide how we will respond? Once more I fear we stand with a glass of water in one hand and a glass of paint thinner in the other.

How do we make decisions as Christians? We are those who have said that Jesus Christ is Lord in our lives, and our primary desire is to know and do His will. We wake up in the morning and say, "Lord, here is my life. What do you want to do today through me?" Isn't that what we say week after week here? You wear your bracelets, W.W.J.D.?, What Would Jesus Do? But I've noticed this week that nobody is asking that question. We really don't want to hear what Jesus would do. We'd really much rather have Joshua or Caleb or Gideon or maybe Samson on our side: Samson, who took the jawbone of an ass and slew a thousand Philistines. We'd rather have Samson than Jesus this week. We don't even ask because we think we know what He might say, He who said, "Love your enemies and pray for those who persecute you. Do good to those who do evil to you, and in this way you'll make known the truth of God." We want vengeance.

So I will be a dissenting voice in everything else you might hear from your friends and family members, maybe even what is welling up in your heart. I had people tell me, "Adam, don't ask this question Sunday. Don't ask this question of the people. The people of the Church of the Resurrection are not ready to hear this question. They're not ready to hear it. They are too angry. They aren't ready to know and ask these kinds of difficult questions."

Here is my fear as your pastor: That by the time you are ready for me to ask this question, it will be too late. So what would Jesus do? What do we want to show the rest of the world? They're watching us. They are watching us rattle our sabers right now, and they're looking to see who we really are and what these Christians in this nation are really made of. So what picture of God will we show them? Now I want you to hear this: I believe that those who perpetrated this crime who are not already dead need to be apprehended and stopped. I believe that there needs to be swift justice and there needs to be firm treatment. I believe that because the scriptures say that while I am to turn the other cheek when somebody hurts me, if someone starts to hurt you, I need to stand between you and that person who's hurting you and protect you. We are called to do that. So if there is a known murderer or rapist and they are murdering and raping, you have a moral obligation as a Christian to stop them from doing that, and if you don't the blood of the innocents is on your hands. So we have a moral obligation to find the people that likely orchestrated this, apprehend them, and, according to the due processes of our laws, take care of this problem.

I fear we have much more in mind than that, so I would ask this question: How many mothers and fathers and sisters and brothers and little children need to die until we feel better about ourselves and what happened this last week? If we kill 5,000 Afghani people, poverty-stricken folks who were not involved in all of this, will that be enough to make us feel better? Or do we need to kill 10,000 to really make our point? What will that say about the American Crusaders? This is a war of ideas; whose ideas should prevail? What makes America great isn't the fact that we could go nuke Afghanistan and totally take out an entire country, though we could. What makes America great is our character. It is our belief in freedom and the due process of law. It is our ability to show restraint instead of showing our power. It is our ability to say we are going to try to do everything that is right and just and fair, and not only react from our hearts. It is our picture of God that is far superior to the picture of a God that believes in the holy *jihad.* That is what makes America great!

Now I would be willing to die in a battle to preserve the lives of other people who are innocents, and if we have to go to war for something like that, then I would do that. But I'm not certain that this is the answer to this situation. Instead, perhaps it would be like pouring something flammable on the flames. So what would it take after apprehending those who are guilty of this crime? What would it take so that all of those others, who stood in line perhaps considering doing the same thing, would be so shamed and humiliated and so clearly see that they were in the wrong that they would not do that? You see Osama bin Laden says, "I'm ready to die. I'm not afraid, they're not afraid to die. Nineteen of them died this last week. I'm not afraid to die. Kill me and there will be 3,000 more rise up in my footsteps." That's what he said. There's got to be another way if we are to wage a war on terrorism, to live a life without it. So I lay that before you. What will they see, America, because the decision really is up to you.

I want to end with these words. Winston Churchill, when he was preparing his nation for invasion by the Nazis, who had already steamrolled over Eastern Europe, was speaking on the radio in an address to a nation that was terrified, and he said, "Be strong and of great courage. We will fight and we will never, ever give up. We will do everything to protect our freedom and our liberties." And then he said this: "Let us brace ourselves to do our duties and so bear ourselves that if the British Empire and Commonwealth lasts for a thousand years, men will say of this time, this was their finest hour."

My hope and dream is that a hundred years from now at the beginning of the twenty-second century, when your great-great-great grandchildren are studying this period of time in humanities class in college, and they are watching it on their DVDs or whatever technology they have, watching the World Trade Center towers collapse, horrified by seeing this thing, when they fast forward and watch what the United States did in the days and weeks following, they will watch that video screen and say, "This was our finest hour."